BASICS
PRODUCT DESIGN

01 Idea Searching

David Bramston

ava | Academia
the environment of learning

An AVA Book

Published by AVA Publishing SA
Rue des Fontenailles 16
Case Postale
1000 Lausanne 6
Switzerland
Tel: +41 786 005 109
Email: enquiries@avabooks.ch

Distributed by Thames & Hudson (ex-North America)
181a High Holborn
London WC1V 7QX
United Kingdom
Tel: +44 20 7845 5000
Fax: +44 20 7845 5055
Email: sales@thameshudson.co.uk
www.thamesandhudson.com

North American Support Office
AVA Publishing
Tel: +1 908 754 6196
Fax: +1 908 668 1172
Email: enquiries@avabooks.ch

English Language Support Office
AVA Publishing (UK) Ltd.
Tel: +44 1903 204 455
Email: enquiries@avabooks.ch

ISBN 2-940373-76-0 and 978-2-940373-76-5
10 9 8 7 6 5 4 3 2 1

Design by Malcolm Southward

Production by
AVA Book Production Pte. Ltd., Singapore
Tel: +65 6334 8173
Fax: +65 6259 9830
Email: production@avabooks.com.sg

All reasonable attempts have been made to trace,
clear and credit the copyright holders of the images
reproduced in this book. However, if any credits
have been inadvertently omitted, the publisher will
endeavour to incorporate amendments in
future editions.

Idea searching

Contents

Idea searching

Contents

Searching for an idea should require all of the senses and should not be a specific activity. The generation of an idea should be a continual process of observing, listening and recording. The eyes and ears are critical tools, but it can be easy to look and not see, and to hear and not listen. Inspiration is everywhere and everything can be inspirational.

There should be a need to share initial thoughts and views with others and to attract as many potential leads for development as possible. In the initial stages of idea generation, everyone is different and everyone has a different take on things. It is important to explore all possible suggestions. It is often the case that an initial proposal for an idea can be misunderstood or taken out of context, but in so doing can trigger stronger ideas and scenarios. There is a need to identify the potential in thoughts and ideas and be prepared to take a risk if there is belief in the suggestion. Individuals who do not take risks with ideas and directions will continue to follow the pack and not lead from the front.

Searching for ideas is obviously a continual process of forming possible solutions and refining these, rather than something that only takes place at the outset of a project.

Experiences are important and these do not need to be specific to the idea that an individual is searching for. Visiting a dog race or attending a ballet may well provide the inspiration necessary for developing a seemingly unrelated project – an individual should always be on the look out for a thought catalyst. Changes in context can enable things to be seen in a different light and perceived in a lateral fashion, rather than a literal one.

'For me design is a question mark. That is how I start every new project.'

<u>Gijs Bakker</u>, 2007

Idea Searching has been developed to explore different pathways for identifying ideas and to understand what is being observed and recorded. The process of searching for ideas often begins with a basic understanding of what is needed. Too much information can be restrictive and can also prevent random thoughts from being given an opportunity to surface. Idea baggage, such as a preconceived notion, can become a mental barrier. An open mind enables thoughts to emerge and develop. Searching for ideas is a process that involves many diverse activities. Brainstorming is often regarded as the initial stage in idea development, but really the process begins much earlier.

The identification of set criteria and themes is an important aspect in the formulation of thoughts and provides direction and boundaries, which if not set out, can lead to a situation that is both unmanageable and without purpose. *Idea Searching* has been divided up into several stages and although these have been presented in a logical order, the purpose of generating ideas is always to question convention and why something is done the way it is. It is therefore possible to refer to different sections of *Idea Searching* and still formulate a reasonable approach.

Idea Searching introduces the subject by exploring areas such as why we do things and observing target groups, activities, and the unconscious actions of others. The need to have empathy with others and not to make assumptions on directions is explored, along with the all-important need to have fun with the design process.

Idea Searching references the approach strategies of many of the leaders in the subject of product/industrial design and the difficulties that can often be encountered in the generation of a 'blue sky' thought through to reality.

'It seems a very dangerous idea. It is – all great ideas are dangerous.'

Oscar Wilde, 1854–1900, De Profundis. A monologue by Oscar Wilde

Andrea Branzi

Andrea Branzi has been a leading architect and designer since the 1960s and has been involved in the development of leading design studios, journals, movements and design schools such as the Domus Academy. He has collaborated with many of the internationally recognised design companies including Vitra, Zanotta and Artemide.

Chapter 1
Just imagine if it were possible
Observations relating to what is actually going on around us and understanding methods for inspiration. Different referencing techniques, the use of scrapbooks, info dumps, notebooks and journals are addressed. Explores questions such as: Why is something done? Why is it the way it is? Why is it needed? What if?

Chapter 2
Common sense is needed
Recognition of empathy in the design process and applying common sense through practical exploration. Examples of product narratives and how design can relate to an individual on a personal level are considered. The importance of boundaries, themes, criteria and objectives are outlined.

Chapter 3
Explore and have fun!
Encourages investigation and exploration with form, scale, texture and materials, aiming to challenge conventional thinking. Innovation, experimentation and fun are essential components of idea searching and are explored using different approaches and techniques.

Chapter 4
Sensory issues
Subtle changes in design can have a significant impact on the way information is perceived. The impact of the senses and the relationship to the design process is introduced and considered. Areas such as product gender, emotion and added values are also explored using examples and case studies.

Chapter 5
Development of an idea
Examines the importance of the refinement of an idea and how to achieve understanding of a product using different critical tools. 'Less is more' is contrasted with visual noise, and the views of product designers in the industry are reflected upon.

Chapter 6
Blue sky or reality?
The issue of the design being a valid proposition is investigated. Areas such as product experiences, brands, and sustainability are explored using a variety of visual examples. The aspect of product logistics is addressed along with the difficulties that still need to be overcome.

Left:
Roppongi Hills street furniture
Streetscape street furniture in Tokyo.

Design:
Andrea Branzi

Photography:
Tom Stott

Introduction > How to get the most out of this book

How to get the most out of this book

This book explores the role that experiences, context, references and the practices of other disciplines play in the generation of effective ideas. The book is divided into six dedicated chapters, each containing a range of examples from contemporary designers and artists, which demonstrate the products that can arise from the effective generation of creative ideas.

Section subheadings
Each section heading is divided into subheadings to provide clear structure and ease of navigation.

'If you have an apple and I have an apple and we exchange these apples then you and I will still each have an apple. But if you have an idea and I have an idea and we exchange these ideas, then each of us will have two ideas.'
George Bernard Shaw, 1856–1950

Brainstorming

An idea can arrive at any time, but it can also be encouraged. It is often thought that the development of an idea is initiated with a brainstorming session: a process where a trigger term is selected and then associations or related analogous themes are communicated.

But such a session relies on individuals having already encountered a diverse range of experiences that are related to the trigger in a direct or indirect manner. The development of an idea usually begins much earlier, although it may remain dormant until there is a suitable verbal or visual catalyst. A brainstorming session is surely, therefore, a vehicle for releasing experiences and stimulating the imagination for future directions or ideas.

Top:
Image wall
The collecting of images to inspire and create a visual environment is an important aspect of the idea searching process.

Middle and bottom:
Artefacts
Objects of interest that fascinate the senses or provide an opening to understand target audience behaviour should be collected and retained within the work environment.

Just imagine if it were possible

Visualstorming

Brainstorming is a verbal process, which involves the identification of key terms associated to an initial idea and the subsequent unleashing of creative directions. It can also be a visual process, which involves the generation of small, thumbnail sketches that are related to, or are tangential to, an idea.

A combination of verbal and visual approaches can often lead to the identification of further triggers, experiences, wish lists, and 'what ifs'. The sharing of observations is critical in a bid to generate as many possible scenarios and directions to explore. An idea, which may sound absurd, may in fact be just the motivating factor needed for another's input into the process. All ideas should be encouraged. A diverse group of individuals will probably bring a broad range of experiences and propositions to recall. Involve everyone.

In the design development process these early ideas are usually critical indicators for future direction. A subconscious sketch, which is often captured in a visual brainstorming session, can often be the key for progression. Giving an idea too much consideration in the initial stages can result in the loss of such pointers. A simple sketch will often capture the essence of what is being considered, whereas a laboured sketch can drive the life and soul of an idea away and leave no room for the imagination to manoeuvre or fill in the gaps. Filling in the gaps and developing bridges with fragments of information provides the opportunity for creativity.

How to?
Using various headings that identify relevant areas to a key theme, the individuals involved in a brainstorming or visualstorming session should aim to communicate all related thoughts using simple terms or images.
All ideas are important at this stage.

Visualstorming
Visualstorming using simple and iconic sketches to communicate fundamental ideas.

Observations > Thoughts

Body text
Supplies an in-depth discussion of the topics covered.

Boxed information
Provides supplementary content in the form of definitions, designer biographies and student exercises.

Chapter navigation
Highlights the current chapter unit and lists previous and following units.

Idea searching

Section headings
Each chapter unit has a clear heading to allow readers to quickly locate an area of interest.

Quotations
Help to place the topic being discussed into context by conveying the views and thoughts of designers and artists.

Referencing

052 **053**

'Drawers are, to me, sensual and mysterious. If you interpret them poetically they enwomb something, nurture and as if giving birth bring it forward.'
Tadao Hoshino, 2007

Product purpose

What is product purpose? The purpose of a product is often isolated as being a physical function, but there is substantially more to the purpose of a product than this particular aspect of function.

Appreciation of functionality needs to be understood at many different levels and not simply the inherent use. Products that are able to combine a variety of functions are capable of appealing to a broader audience. Beauty, fun and brand awareness are some of the functions that may be associated with a design in addition to the practical elements.

headstand grp°
Understanding the purpose of a product is a fundamental aspect in achieving a successful design. The headstand grp° stool designed by qed° manages to instantly capture the imagination and demand respect through its combined awareness of fun and creativity.

Design:
qed° – Michael Neubauer and Matthias Wieser

Aphrodite
The Aphrodite drawer system manages to defy expectation, questions user experiences and captivates the observer by its unquestionable elegance, grace and physical beauty.

Design:
Tadao Hoshino – Edition Ligne Roset

Photography:
Shuya Sato

Just imagine if it were possible

Thoughts > Referencing

Captions
Provide contextual information about the products displayed.

Images
Examples from contemporary designers and artists bring principles under discussion to life.

Introduction > How to get the most out of this book > Just imagine if it were possible

'Imagination is more important than knowledge.
Knowledge is limited. Imagination encircles the world.'

Albert Einstein, 1929

The ability to observe is important.
Not to watch, but to observe. How do
individuals actually interact with their
environments and do they make
modifications to products that were
intended to be used in a certain way?

Observational triggers are often
necessary to identify a possible
direction and can occur anywhere
and at anytime. Triggers may be
subconscious observations or
deliberate choices. No observation,
no stimulation, no imagination.

The question to ask is, why?
Observing, questioning, listening and
interpreting. Images and artefacts that
are collected are invaluable as a source
of inspiration and can prompt further
discussion and direction.

droog

Gijs Bakker co-founded
droog with Renny Ramakers
in 1993. The design work of
droog has challenged
conventional approaches to
design and has resulted in
many innovative products.

Left:
Tokyo Day-tripper
Streetscape street furniture in
Tokyo.

Design:
Rianne Makkink and Jürgen Bey

Observations

'If you have an apple and I have an apple and we exchange these apples then you and I will still each have an apple. But if you have an idea and I have an idea and we exchange these ideas, then each of us will have two ideas.'

George Bernard Shaw, 1856–1950

Brainstorming

An idea can arrive at any time, but it can also be encouraged. It is often thought that the development of an idea is initiated with a brainstorming session: a process where a trigger term is selected and then associations or related analogous themes are communicated.

But such a session relies on individuals having already encountered a diverse range of experiences that are related to the trigger in a direct or indirect manner. The development of an idea usually begins much earlier, although it may remain dormant until there is a suitable verbal or visual catalyst. A brainstorming session is surely, therefore, a vehicle for releasing experiences and stimulating the imagination for future directions or ideas.

Top:
Image wall
The collecting of images to inspire and create a visual environment is an important aspect of the idea searching process.

Middle and bottom:
Artefacts
Objects of interest that fascinate the senses or provide an opening to understand target audience behaviour should be collected and retained within the work environment.

Just imagine if it were possible

Visualstorming

Brainstorming is a verbal process, which involves the identification of key terms associated to an initial idea and the subsequent unleashing of creative directions. It can also be a visual process, which involves the generation of small, thumbnail sketches that are related to, or are tangential to, an idea.

A combination of verbal and visual approaches can often lead to the identification of further triggers, experiences, wish lists, and 'what ifs'. The sharing of observations is critical in a bid to generate as many possible scenarios and directions to explore. An idea, which may sound absurd, may in fact be just the motivating factor needed for another's input into the process. All ideas should be encouraged. A diverse group of individuals will probably bring a broad range of experiences and propositions to recall. Involve everyone.

In the design development process these early ideas are usually critical indicators for future direction. A subconscious sketch, which is often captured in a visual brainstorming session, can often be the key for progression. Giving an idea too much consideration in the initial stages can result in the loss of such pointers. A simple sketch will often capture the essence of what is being considered, whereas a laboured sketch can drive the life and soul of an idea away and leave no room for the imagination to manoeuvre or fill in the gaps. Filling in the gaps and developing bridges with fragments of information provides the opportunity for creativity.

How to?

Using various headings that identify relevant areas to a key theme, the individuals involved in a brainstorming or visualstorming session should aim to communicate all related thoughts using simple terms or images.

All ideas are important at this stage.

Visualstorming

Visualstorming using simple and iconic sketches to communicate fundamental ideas.

Thumbnails

A thumbnail sketch is a visual representation that is unpretentious and aims to capture the essence of a proposal or idea.
The depiction is usually considered and the result of a conscious thought, unlike a doodle, which tends to be less intentional and more abstract – the result of a subconscious or absent mind. The scribbles and marks of a doodle need to be carefully placed in context due to their transcendental nature. It may be interesting, but it is unlikely to be as beneficial as a thumbnail interpretation of an idea, as concentration was not applied when it was produced.

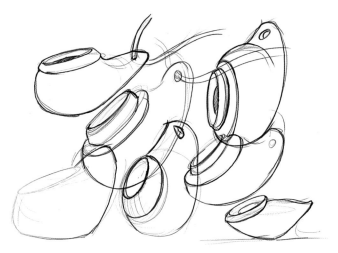

Thumbnail
A simple thumbnail sketch of a possible cellphone. The visual thought manages to capture the essence of a direction without being too refined.

Mind *n*. The faculty of consciousness and thought.

Thumbnail *n*. Brief or concise in description or representation.

Doodle *v*. Scribble absent-mindedly.

Just imagine if it were possible

Scenarios

The development of an idea can be explored using mixed media, which provides further stimulation and an opportunity to probe the narrative. The use of mixed media is a technique that is employed by photographers, artists and designers, and involves the use of different materials, media and approaches to create a stimulating image.

Chiaroscuro is a technique in painting where emphasis is placed on the light and dark regions. The use of chiaroscuro usually involves a shaft of light targeting the subject matter whilst surrounding elements are placed into shadow.

Found objects, which have a basic affinity with the general components of an idea, can be used to develop a representation of a proposal and assist in capturing an understanding of the form. It is often difficult to comprehend the physical presence of an idea in a mental state and simplistic scenarios can assist significantly. Artistic licence can present bias and ultimately avoid issues that should be addressed, resulting in time being wasted if an idea is not subjected to scrutiny in a physical context. The use of black-and-white photography to capture an idea in context can provide a suitable image to investigate using mixed media. A form of chiaroscuro can be adopted to emphasise specific elements of the object.

 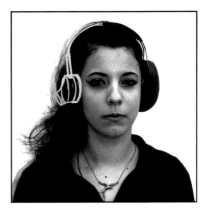

Headsets
Development of headset using mixed media: photograph and pen.

chiaro: light
scuro: dark

The French term *grisaille* refers to a method where painting is executed in monochrome and is therefore closely associated to the chiaroscuro approach.

Observations > Thoughts

Montage

A visual montage relates to the positioning together of different images or forms from various origins to create an enhanced or more influential method of communication than the individual items presented separately. Due to the composition being produced from various sources there is a tendency for scale, form and texture to vary throughout the work, thus providing opportunity for viewer interpretation and association. A montage is in many respects a compilation of observations; a visual story utilising different references and aimed at projecting feeling. The production of a montage is a complicated task, with balance, weight, and relationships to other elements within the work requiring consideration.

A montage is not intended to be understood in a literal sense, but perhaps more in an intellectual and philosophical sense. The montage should provide an opportunity to create an atmosphere or impression of an idea, rather than to dictate it.

A photomontage is usually compiled through a series of photographs taken from the same location and records vertical and horizontal aspects compiled into a panoramic, patchwork image.

A composite facsimile can also be produced if the subject matter remains static and photographs are taken around the subject matter.

The photomontage is useful at capturing a generic scene and provides opportunity for imagination to interpret the narrative of the complete work.

Top:
Panoramic photomontage of Tokyo skyline
The sweeping view is obtained by splicing together a number of images. The individual shots were taken looking at different aspects of the city from the same vantage point.

Bottom:
Montage
The montage uses fragments of sourced images to communicate a theme associated to personal finance. The composition aims to communicate the transition from monetary chaos to an organised state in personal banking.

Just imagine if it were possible

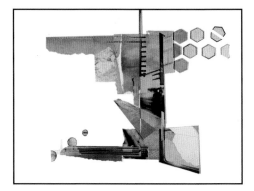

Role play

Role play is the simulation of a story and provides an opportunity to engage in a situation to develop physical and/or mental empathy. The activity is essentially an opportunity to directly relate and interact with a problem or an idea; a performance to understand the bigger picture. The practice provides an alternative and simple way to understand issues and can identify directions which may not have been evident had the problem been approached in a logical and inert manner.

Mental role play can be conducted at any time by viewing a particular activity in the mind or in conjunction with minor movements and sound. Physical role play – the actual acting out of a situation – needs to be approached in a space that is representative of an environment, and requires imagination and creativity. The ability to adopt roles and characters and utilise experiences is important. Physical resources can be symbolic as a general reference to an item is often sufficient to understand the key issues.

Role play
Role play was used here to understand constraints and opportunities in the administration of first aid.

'It's not what you look at that matters, it's what you see.'

Henry David Thoreau, 1817–1862

Just imagine if it were possible

Modifications

Everyday situations provide an
opportunity to trigger inspiration
and reference ideas. Inspiration
is everywhere.

Modifications

As the lamp post is only used for its intended function during the hours of darkness, it is important that it can be identified to have other objectives, whether intentional or not. These could include: supporting road signs; attachment of traffic lights; locking bikes to; tethering animals; securing flags; providing vantage points; as crash barriers; sticking flyers to; bus stops; perches for birds; supporting telephone cables; meeting points and to light an area during darkness.

There are many examples of products being used for ways that they were perhaps not originally intended. Observing such modifications can provide direction for the development of these products. A lamp post could be developed to project a shadow of a street name or direction to a nearby street or station. Lamp posts could perhaps be colour coded to represent different speed limits or districts. It is important to make a physical or mental note of such adaptations when they are seen so as to provide inspiration at the idea stage.

Tokyo and New York
Lamp posts used in a variety
of ways.

Observations > Thoughts

'If you are in a shipwreck and all the boats are gone, a piano top buoyant enough to keep you afloat may come along and make a fortuitous life preserver. This is not to say though, that the best way to design a life preserver is in the form of a piano top.'

R. Buckminster Fuller, Operating Manual for Spaceship Earth, 1963

The different ways that existing products are used can provide useful insights for further ideas; insights are merely suggestions and not solutions.

Hair clip > Bookmarker
Coat hanger > Car aerial
Tin of paint > Doorstop
Stool > Steps
Blanket > Rope
Tin can > Cup
Glass bottle > Rolling pin
Newspaper > Fly swat
Jam jar > Fish tank
Box > Home
Bucket > Net
CD > Decoration
Balloon > Water container
Frying pan > Baseball bat
Rock > Mallet
Paperback book > Fan
Ladder > Bridge
School jumper > Goalpost
Chalk stick > Weapon
Ice cream tub > Bait box
Bin bag > Anorak
Tray > Snowboard

Saw > Instrument
Stockings > Mask
Rug > Den
Paper > Hat
Football > Swimming float
Paintbrush > Duster
Traffic cone > Table leg
Bin > Toy storage
Gate > Bench
Paper cup > Ashtray
Paper plate > Pizza holder
Shoebox > Memory case
Umbrella > Sun shield
Car tyres > Crash barriers
Concrete wall > Chair
Fridge > Noticeboard
Car key > Scribe
Toothbrush > Shoe cleaner
Pebbles > Paperweights
Table > Raft
Wire fence > Tennis net
Sleeve > Handkerchief
Metal railings > Horse tether
Comb > Instrument
Supermarket trolley > Go-cart
Bed > Trampoline
Napkin > Sketchbook

Plastic bags > Sterile shoes
Airbed > Windshield
Broom > Paintbrush
Plant pot > Spider trap
Skateboard > Furniture trolley
Wallet > Photo album
Bin > Goal
Large book > Flower press
Watering can > Shower
Cardboard tube > Sword
House brick > Hammer
Hedgerow stile > Chair
Car spark plug > Fishing weight
Torch > Club
Size 10 slippers > Fly swat
Garden spade > Seat
Tennis racket > Sieve
Fallen tree > Bridge
Folded cardboard > Door wedge
Beer mat > Table stabiliser
Pudding Bowl > Scoop
Spoons > Musical instrument
Sticky tape > Clothes brush
Bottle lid > Measure
Fire > Torch
Scarf > Restraint
Brooch > Fastener
Bedroom pillow > Weapon
Broom > Prop
Cap > Tray
Park hedge > Barrier

Just imagine if it were possible

Broken bottle > Match
Size 12 boot > Hammer
Magazine stack > Stool
Friend's back > Desk
Ribbon > Barrier
Tie > Belt
Table > Shelter
Cabinet > Plinth
Mug > Penholder
Open newspaper > Umbrella
School bag > Pillow
Towel > Rug
Old jeans > Notebook
Window > Message board
Paddling pool > Fridge
Pram > Trolley
Chair > Table leg
Suitcase > Seat
Handbag > Dance partner
Bus stop > Bed
Spade > Paddle
Saucer > Key storage
Glass beaker > Amplifier
Plastic plate > Fan
Large tree > Umbrella
Chair back > Coat hanger
Window > Mirror
Pen > Cigarette
Coin > Tin opener
Handkerchief > Sun hat
Metal tray > Bat
Coat > Filing cabinet
Paper clip > Key
Sandpit > Cup holder
Cap > Ball catcher

Milk bottle > Vase
Old boot > Flowerpot
Bottle > Candleholder
Hood > Basket
Shopping bags > Panniers
Pallet > Fencing
Tree > Toilet
Bicycle handlebars > Bag carriers
Chimney > Plant pot
Milk crate > Seating
Pen > Drumstick
Car roof > Picnic table
Drinks can > Football
Folded newspaper > Tray
Oil drum > Coffee table
Road > Ashtray
Toilet roll > Notepad
Socks > Gloves
Lipstick > Marker pen
Bag > Dog basket
Concrete slab > Anchor
Cushion > Crash pad
Bricks > Car jack
Pillow > Prop
Stairs > Seating
Drinking glass > Magnifier
Ear > Penholder
Table > Footrest
Violin case > Collection box
Flat cap > Collection pot
Fire extinguisher > Doorstop
Plastic bottle > Buoy
Surfboard > Stretcher
Coat > Blanket
Balloon > Location marker
Bathtub > Boat
Bin lid > Shield
Margarine tub > Dog bowl
Suitcase > Wardrobe
Books > Steps
Towel > Privacy screen
Egg box > Insulation
Jam jar > Cup

Sink > Planter
Door > Skate ramp
Credit card > Ice scraper
Tractor tyres > Mini roundabout
Kerb > Bike stand
Step > Shoe cleaner
Knife > Screwdriver
Log pile > Seating
Handrail > Slide
Pencil > Hole punch

Buckminster Fuller

Buckminster Fuller, 1895–1983, was a designer, futurist and writer who focused predominantly on the issue of how the human race could endure the potential problems it was facing and secure existence on earth. As an individual he aimed to demonstrate how it was possible to embrace some of the issues the world needed to engage with that were not being confronted by the larger organisations. The publication *Operating Manual for Spaceship Earth* (1963) portrayed earth as a spaceship with limited resources that could not be replaced. The metaphor acutely demonstrated the need for everyone to consider carefully his or her destination.

Observations > Thoughts

User refinements

Although many products are mass-produced it is often the case that the item has been developed in such a way as to give the impression that it is unique to the user. Despite achieving the feeling of belonging to the user many individuals will still make adjustments to the design. Alterations may appear to be abstract and occasionally bizarre however, the owner has felt it necessary, for whatever reason, to execute the changes no matter how small. It is important to observe such alterations and to evaluate why they have been conducted. There may be many reasons to warrant changes including sentimental, practical and desire. Exploring and understanding these user refinements can assist in developing a product.

User refinements
User refinements including attachment of tags, scratched identity and a directory.

Refinement *n*. An improvement.

Just imagine if it were possible

Primary research
Primary research involves obtaining information from source, such as interviewing skateboarders to find out related information.

Primary research

Understanding or identifying a problem usually requires an activist 'go do' approach to make important connections and place them in context. It is necessary not to be judgemental, biased, or to have preconceived ideas, but to retain an open mind and be prepared to appreciate outcomes.

Primary research can be conducted utilising a diverse range of methods including interviewing, shadowing a target group, adopting a character, or random sampling. Stories and analogous responses can provide valuable detail, which may not surface without interaction. It is preferable to capture information for subsequent analysis using audio or visual methods.

Observations > Thoughts

User research

Understanding a user and his or her behaviour can be enhanced through simple investigative methods. The contents of a person's pockets can be very revealing and can provide much valuable information – providing that they are prepared to share it. A pocket can contain numerous artefacts that are obviously personal and of sufficient value to be transported on the individual. The pocket contents are non-judgemental and will reveal personal habits, issues and agendas. Items from several days, weeks or even years ago can be identified and influence directional thinking. Analysing particular relationships between items in conjunction with the user provides a valuable impression that might not be fully obtainable through observation alone.

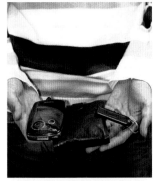

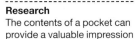

Research
The contents of a pocket can provide a valuable impression of a character.

Just imagine if it were possible

Stories and listening

A story can be told verbally, visually, or through a combination of both, and is capable of capturing an audience through detail in expression, vocal emphasis, descriptive terminology, metaphors and body language. It requires the listener, reader or observer to make a connection, to form an alliance and to contextualise the meaning. A story provides opportunity for imagination and empathy, with gaps and pauses being left for interpretation, realism and possible affinity to individual experiences.

The use of visual triggers such as body language, facial expression, imagery or setting, assists in the projection and understanding and should be observed carefully to provide direction. The voice of experience is important in acquiring the context of a problem and although issues may sometimes be over-emphasised or exaggerated, the fundamentals of the message are usually accurate indicators for consideration. A story that is retold is often a different story and a story that is told through many voices is capable of encompassing a wider range of issues and structures.

The listener has an important role in the understanding of a story, as not to listen carefully or not to recognise a hidden detail can result in misunderstanding, confusion, and blurring.

**New York busker
at Ground Zero**
The stories that are evident in the image are numerous and yet may not be fully appreciated by simply passing by the street busker. Is there a direct relationship between the busker and the venue? What is the busker's song, message or story? It is necessary to look and listen to understand context and meaning.

The match seller New York
An individual's story can be told visually and/or verbally and should be observed and/or listened to carefully.

Inspiration

An architectural reclaim yard can provide valuable inspiration for different approaches to design. It is important to think about objects with an open mind and consider how they may influence an idea rather than simply be reproduced.

Taking objects out of context and exploring their potential can lead to exciting developments that break away from the mundane and the conventional. An unorthodox examination of items within the reclaim yard can provide a beneficial stimulus that is often not accessible without looking carefully. The patterns that such varied objects can present can be exciting and it is necessary to imagine the items at a different scale or in a different material.

An item should not be categorised because of history; it should be thought of in different contexts and environments. It is also useful not just to simply explore the obvious items, but to look closely at the relationships between items or the way in which the 'rejected' artefacts have been set out.

It is not always possible to know what to look for and what to dismiss and, although initial instinct can be a reasonable indicator, it is advisable that everything is noted, both physically and mentally.

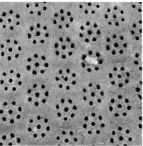

Just imagine if it were possible

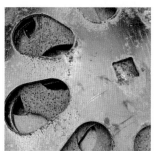

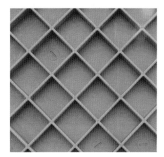

- -

Radiator inspiration
A random collection of selected
items at an architectural reclaim
yard that offer something to the
imagination during the initial
stages of radiator research. None
of the selected items were former
radiators, but all stimulated
interest.

Jumper goal posts
Children are amongst the most
creative of individuals as they
tend not to be too judgemental
and are often content with an
interpretation of an idea at a basic
level. The use of jumpers, bags
or coats as makeshift goal posts
for an impromptu game of
football is a familiar site on
playing fields and other
recreational spaces. The absence
of a vertical post, net or cross
bar becomes insignificant as the
game gets underway.

Just imagine if it were possible

Improvisation

Observing how individuals interact within their environments provides a good pointer to the sort of products that could be developed. Situations where there are limited resources available, such as camping, the beach and park visits, often result in compromise and innovation.

Tennis-net park fence
If a game of tennis is sought, the issue of not having the correct equipment can sometimes become a minor detail. Representation of what is needed will often suffice, especially as the real purpose of the game is to have time with friends. A park fence that is almost the size of the players is no longer a problem as it will do to get the activity underway. No boundaries to the court, incorrect clothing and probably no real understanding of the rules all become irrelevant. The objective is simply to have fun. Improvisation allows for rules to be broken and imagination to emerge.

Brief

The design brief usually relates to the engagement of a project and can be presented in a formal or informal fashion. It is not necessarily the initiation of the thinking process, as observations, thoughts and experiences should always be ongoing.

The important issue is to actually understand what is being communicated and to be prepared to investigate hidden detail, which might not be apparent to others. The designer must be able to respond to what is being requested positively and with creativity, but also prompt lateral lines of enquiry through questioning.

The language used can often be an obstacle that needs to be negotiated carefully. In the situation where a product is required for a particular market the terminology used can instigate a series of creative responses or subject the project to unnecessary boundaries.

A 'drinks flask' is a 'drinks vessel' however, if the former description is used the responses are perhaps likely to be more constrained as the immediate thought is of a cylindrical container. The 'drinks vessel' terminology does not prejudge and is therefore without creative baggage.

Drinks vessel or drinks flask?
The terminology that is used to describe something can appear to be similar but can actually lead to significantly different outcomes.

Brief *adj*. Of short duration. Concise; using few words.

Language can be manipulated effectively to generate thoughts and conjure up ideas. The name of a simple product such as a lunch box could be replaced with alternative words or slang that befits the target audience in an attempt to address possible lines of enquiry. For example: scoff sack; troff tray; bite bag; scram jar; snack pack; fodder file; pud pod; mess case; grub trunk; ration wrap; scoop crate; snaffle sock; tuc tub; chow caddy.

It is not uncommon for individuals to produce their own lunch boxes from margarine or ice cream containers, or from foil or brown paper bags. The manner in which such containers are modified and personalised can provide a direction to consider.

Lunch containers
These self-made lunch containers convey personality traits.

> 'The idea generating process never stops for me; the ideas flow continuously. That is the easy part. The hard part is making the idea real.'
>
> **Angela Yoder**, 2008

Variations

Understanding and thinking about how problems are addressed with home-made products provides a valuable insight into what the user is wanting and offers an opportunity to improve or refine these simple versions. The range of home-made products – solutions developed by the user for the user – is broad and should be acknowledged.

Brown paper bag lunch containers may become insulated containers with opportunities for name tags and personalisation. Ice cream cartons can inspire practical storage solutions for lunches and be enhanced with hard and soft zone dividers, or areas that might segregate smells. The foil-wrapped sandwich with an elastic band to hold it together may develop into a wrapper, which can double up to form a place mat or provide the impetus for a cloth or napkin.

Observing different styles and variations of home-made lunch containers can also provide an insight into what kinds of food an individual is eating and the context of where it is being eaten. Do different styles apply to different occasions? Are alterations made to accommodate something not normally associated with a lunch container? If given the opportunity would a user of a lunch container want to include hot items?

The range of food normally included in a lunch container is somewhat limited with pre-packed and cold items being the primary contents. What about a hot pudding or perhaps a hot dog? How could this be accommodated? Asking a target group what they take and why, can reveal that what they do isn't what they want. Involving a target group in what is needed or what they would ideally take provides the opportunity to explore ideas.

In addition to home-made products there are numerous examples of food being packaged for on-the-move experiences. The packaging from fast food restaurants, including polystyrene trays, paper or card boxes, can inform an ideas process. Considering take-away packaging from restaurants and airline food trays may also provide inspiration and enable possibilities to be explored.

How to?

To understand a particular problem it is advisable to try and encounter it. The issue of packed lunches has been tackled frequently and there is a diverse range of products available for the consumer.

Why are packed lunches often seen as a stopgap meal, a snack, rather than a real enjoyable experience? Look at the amount of food that is taken in different lunch containers, and if anything else is included such as a mat or cutlery.

Just imagine if it were possible

Margarine tub inspired lunch box

Considering self-made lunch containers from simple packaging, such as ice cream or margarine cartons, can inspire ideas. The use of stickers on such items work well as they are easily changed by the consumer or manufacturer when a fashion changes.

Dos Chicas © Lorraine Lunch Bag

Design:
Angela Yoder

Mental baggage

An experience can be a particularly useful tool, but overexposure to something can develop an individual's mental baggage. When mental baggage is prevalent it can be difficult to consider any other creative direction other than that of the overfamiliar, and it can be arduous to persuade others to explore an alternative path when they also have a preconceived notion of what the product is. It is only when things can be thought of differently, without accustomed barriers, that it is plausible to innovate markets. If the problem is not confronted with a 'why attitude', similar to a small child constantly asking questions about something, it is almost impossible to understand and develop. In the event that mental baggage can be broken down through repeated enquiry and probing, it is likely that a delightful and practical proposal can emerge and be accepted broadly.

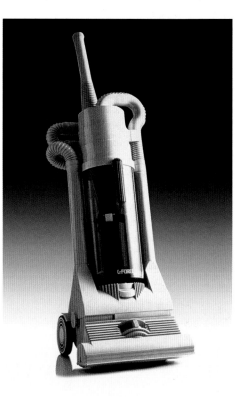

The G Force bagless vacuum cleaner, designed by James Dyson was initially sold in Japan. Dyson had questioned the accepted standards of a vacuum cleaner. The ability to ask the basic questions and to ignore convention and mental baggage is at the heart of good design. Dyson continues to ask why and continues to manoeuvre around preconceived ideas and boundaries to remain innovative.

G Force
James Dyson's G Force vacuum cleaner. The functionality of the design differed on many levels to its predecessors and in 1991 won the Japanese International Design Fair prize.

Just imagine if it were possible

Good and bad design

Is it possible to say that a design is good or bad? Appreciation of a design is surely subjective with some individuals expressing a desire for an item, whilst others a dislike, or simply disapproval at its difference. It is probably impossible to get everyone to agree on whether a design is good or bad from a subjective standpoint.

Perhaps it is possible to categorise an object as being good or bad on the basis of function and fit for purpose? Providing it is apparent what the function actually is – this, unfortunately, is not always as straightforward as it may initially appear. Function can be ambiguous and can be sectioned under numerous headings relating to the overall design. A cheap watch and an expensive watch both function as timekeepers, but certainly also have other functions such as representing a certain behaviour, conduct, attitude and brand.

Maybe a design can only be critically evaluated if placed in the context of the initial objective, where constraints are understood – but would subjective opinion remain?

The Polyprop chair
The Polyprop chair demonstrates that good design can be practical, inexpensive, lasting and beautiful.

Design:
The original Polyprop chair (1962–1963) was designed by Robin Day for Hille International UK

Observations > **Thoughts** > Referencing

Analogous

The referencing of similar objects or systems is useful when addressing particular issues or problems. An analogous item may be targeted at a completely different audience or may appear to be unrelated. However, investigation will reveal that there are relationships, which might be influential and provide direction. The search for analogous products is simple if items can be taken out of context and seen differently.

The various features of a laptop that require consideration might include portability, ability to fold up, the screen characteristic and the manner in which information can be input. Understanding competitors and rival products does provide valuable information, but may not provide opportunity to innovate the market. A review of seemingly unrelated products, which perhaps have a single aspect in common, can ignite alternative ideas.

To consider portability for a laptop the analogous products that could be considered might be a portable television or radio as these will have similar traits. The issue of folding might involve exploring items such as newspapers or towels, leading to a pathway that considers total flexibility or perhaps a laptop that could be rolled up?

Exploring books or a diary layout might instigate a line of thought that proposes multiple screens, which can be flipped over or similar. The idea of inputting information might take reference from historical products such as a typewriter or calculator. Analogous products are extremely beneficial at exploring alternative opportunities for conventional products and should always be considered.

Just imagine if it were possible

Analogous *adj*. Comparable in certain respects.

Analogy *n*. A comparison between one thing and another made for the purpose of explanation or clarification.

TV > Laptop

A portable television is a possible analogous product to consider if thinking about the portability of an item. In the generation of initial proposals for a laptop the television is likely to have certain attributes that may be worth recognising. Areas such as integral handle, balance and scale may be a few of the issues where intelligence could be sourced.

TV > Laptop

The portable television is generally accepted as being a simple product for a particular target market. The simplicity, robust qualities and overall structure of the television may provide further inspiration in the initial stages of proposal for a product such as a laptop. Analogous products are tried and tested and provide a wealth of information.

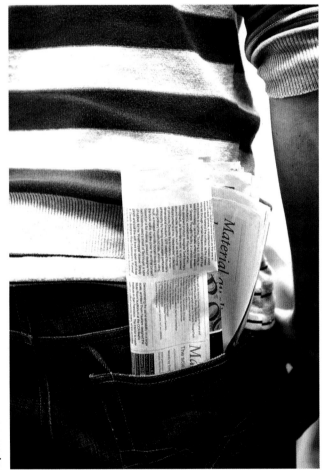

Newspaper > Laptop
Observing how individuals interact with everyday objects is necessary in establishing user habits and relationships. A newspaper that is casually rolled up and placed in a back pocket might inspire a theme or direction for an emerging product. Why can't a laptop be rolled up and treated in such a personal fashion? Does anything actually prevent the laptop being treated in such a way? Is a flexible laptop possible?

Just imagine if it were possible

Above and right:
Typewriter > Laptop
There is a multitude of different input devices that could possibly inspire thinking and the development of a laptop.
The typewriter is the recognised ancestor of the laptop and although technology has advanced, such products may still have something that might capture the imagination.
The angled keyboard or the sculptured form of the keys may provide some inspiration.

Mood board

Reference material is often selected to set a scene or an atmosphere at the outset of the design process. The purpose is to inspire, to capture the essence of a desired direction, a feeling or an intention. It may reflect a given emotion or poignant expression, but it can also provide a visual opportunity to consider generic issues such as texture and scale.

The images should have the capability to ignite thinking amongst observers, to trigger recall and provide mental connections with previous activities. The mood board can consist of a single image or an array of images projecting a simple message.

Mood boards
A message relating to movement is captured using imagery from Tokyo. The mood board aims to set a path for a desired line of thinking.

Just imagine if it were possible

Ceremony

Ceremony can be defined as a distinct procedure, a performance that adheres to protocols and rules. A ceremony can often adopt a theatrical characteristic and is reserved either for special occasions or for creating a sensation of importance. Although usually associated with religious experiences, rituals are encountered all the time and are often conducted or acted out subconsciously by an individual or group.

A barber sets out scissors, combs, blades and other essential equipment in a configuration that ensures that the customer experience and the actual task of cutting hair are distinctive and appropriate.

A trader, set up to clean shoes of passers-by in the street, lays out a stall with an array of brushes, clothes, waxes and laces to perform a service and generate an experience for the customer.

The surgeon lines up scalpels, dishes, swabs, knives and other essential implements to perform an operation in a particular way.

A cup of tea can be prepared carefully, following familiar methods, with attention being given to every detail. The complete process can adopt a ceremonial aspect enhancing the overall experience.

The barber ceremony
The laying out of equipment in a formal manner suggests a certain professionalism that is both encouraging to the customer and beneficial to the user. The process may possibly be part theatre, but it is important and should be noted.

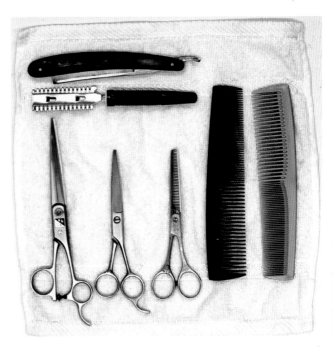

Thoughts > Referencing

2pm?

Simple cameras or any other method of recording events can be utilised to great effect to provide information that assists in understanding the context of a situation.

A camera can be used to record the circumstances that an individual is in when they hear a particular sound or piece of music. It can be used to record events that are taking place at a set time during the day, or to capture the environment when something is eaten.

Although the procedure may appear mundane, the outcomes are often unexpected and surprising. Preconceived ideas are frequently challenged and shown to be inaccurate and misguiding.

The visual record may show that the majority of food consumed during a 24-hour period is actually eaten away from a recognised dining environment and outside of an assumed time frame. The information recorded may detail that cellphone calls are often received at a time when it is difficult to respond or hear.

Capturing events as they occur is important and difficult to contradict. The visual record of circumstance is a useful tool.

When a ring is heard
Identifying a particular sound or noise and recording your situation every time it is heard can provide some intriguing information.

Location at 2pm
An individual's perception of what they do during 24 hours and what they actually do can be surprisingly inaccurate. Identifying a set time such as 2pm and recording what is directly in front of them at that point will reveal much information and draw attention to what is really going on.

Just imagine if it were possible

Adore

I like it, I want it, what is it? The reasoning
behind why somebody 'likes' something can
be simple to comprehend, but can also be
complex and difficult to rationalise. A trendy
'must have' material may be adored by the
user, as it is believed that ownership
improves quality of life – a fundamental aim
of design. However, a small, grubby, pink
blanket or an apparently insignificant, tatty
bracelet may be loved by their owner as
both are associated to times gone by, such
as childhood, with fond memories becoming
more embellished as time passes by. It is
not possible to guess if an item is adored by
simply observing or thinking about it. The
product needs to be placed in the correct
situation, and what one person worships
may be regarded as insignificant or peculiar
to others.

Adore
It is not uncommon for individuals
to lavish attention on what often
appear to others to be worthless,
inanimate objects. Love and
affection are given to seemingly
random and obscure objects, but
there is often a significant
sentimental or personal reason
which cannot be broken with
these items.

Thoughts > Referencing

Scrapbook

A scrapbook is an important, but often underrated, tool within the process of gaining inspiration. The scrapbook should be developed continually with visual representations, collected items and other artefacts of interest. There are no rules apart from collect anything and everything that strikes a creative chord. The aim of the scrapbook is to catalogue memories and experiences so that it is possible to summon events to mind effectively at a later date.

The ability to recall and conjure up personal encounters stimulates further awareness of a situation and can trigger responses from individuals who were not privileged to be present when the original record was produced, but who are able to call to mind similar exposure.

The scrapbook requires continual care and maintenance to ensure that sourced information does not get damaged and that emerging areas of interest are represented. It is often the case that the more unusual or abstract the entry is to a scrapbook, the more interesting it will become.

Memories *n*. The faculty by which the mind stores and remembers information.

Sketchbook and notebook

The sketchbook and notebook can work effectively in conjunction with each other, providing that sketches can capture the essence of what is being viewed, and the notebook can record it accurately and concisely. A few simple marks or key words can often record elements that a more sophisticated method of recording would not be able to do. The strength of a line or a metaphor can place an observation with surprising detail, which can be referenced at a later stage with considerable accuracy.

Left and right:
Scrapbook
Formulating a scrapbook is in many respects a personal and organic process. Items of interest, which may or may not be directly related to a current project, should be included. The development of a scrapbook needs to be ongoing, capturing experiences and constantly recording. Innovation sometimes needs to be employed regarding the acceptance of large items into the collection, but it is important to include as much as possible.

A library of scrapbooks from personal experiences is a very valuable resource.

Info dump

In the search for original directions it is necessary to track down the unknown. Items which are unfamiliar and removed from the everyday can be a valuable source of inspiration. It is not a simple process to identify what will provide stimulation or incentive for a particular product so it is better to conduct a broad sweep of everything that is exciting visually, and to deliberate over the positives and negatives at a later stage. A collected item may be of interest because of a single facet and should not be rejected because this facet is not regarded as sufficient; it could be the catalyst that is needed in the development process.

Areas that often provide particular interest include vending machines, market stalls, or shops that offer an element of intrigue through a diversity of eclectic items. The ability to explore such outlets in different countries frequently results in peculiar items being discovered, which demand attention and immediately present a spectrum of ideas.

The info dump is the informal process of presenting the collected imagery and artefacts to a receptive audience capable of constructive criticism.

Searching the unfamiliar
Charity shops, market stalls, vending machines and unusual shops, which are removed from mainstream trends, can provide important inspiration for an info dump.

Just imagine if it were possible

Journals

Journals provide a valuable source of contemporary reference material, which allows an understanding of what is occurring to be accessed effectively and efficiently. Journals targeted at the creative disciplines outside of the sphere of product design, and often beyond the realm of design completely, can also frequently provide an insight to very relevant issues. Business and science journals provide a significant amount of information that is creative, inspiring and enlightening, and should not be overlooked in a quest to be innovative. It is not uncommon for many of the leading design offices to subscribe to such journals and source further information from outlets such as Reuters and Bloomberg.

The designer needs to be a sponge for information and needs to be able to explore, analyse and categorise as frequently as possible.

Journals
International design journals provide a valuable source of background knowledge, direction and inspiration. A journal that is published in a foreign language can still provide much visual stimulation. Design is a visual process.

'Nothing is a waste of time if you use the experience wisely.'

Rodin, French sculptor 1840–1917

Experiences

Experiences are important to generate ideas. Without experiences it is difficult to contextualise, and being unable to contextualise a situation or idea can lead to a lack of direction or thought. An experience does not need to be undertaken in an elaborate setting, it just requires enquiry, enthusiasm, conviction and a desire to understand. The experience being conducted may be abstract to an outcome, but will almost certainly influence a thought if given the opportunity to do so. A specific element of the experience, a texture or perhaps an appreciation of balance, might just be the necessary stimulant needed to investigate and interpret the problem from an alternative perspective.

An opportunity to attend a glass studio, a theatre production or visit an unknown culture should, if possible, be taken up to broaden horizons and mental resources for idea generation.

Do something different as often as possible.

Experimental Wobbly Bowl
Understanding materials and interacting with them directly is an important facet of the design process. A willingness to experience the unknown provides an essential mental resource.

Design:
Colin Brown; The National Glass Centre, Sunderland, UK

How to

Design requires experiences and some are adopted unknowingly whilst others are planned. Aim to attend a different event as often as possible. Simple experiences, such as drinking a cup of tea at a different venue each day, provide a wealth of experiences and an insight into different cultures.

Just imagine if it were possible

The manipulation of glass
Colin Brown at the National Glass
Centre demonstrates the process
of producing the Wobbly Bowl.
Observing and experiencing such
events should be an ongoing
process and an aspect which
inspires and drives creativity.

'Drawers are, to me, sensual and mysterious. If you interpret them poetically they enwomb something, nurture and as if giving birth bring it forward.'

Tadao Hoshino, 2007

Product purpose

What is product purpose? The purpose of a product is often isolated as being a physical function, but there is substantially more to the purpose of a product than this particular aspect of function.

Appreciation of functionality needs to be understood at many different levels and not simply the inherent use. Products that are able to combine a variety of functions are capable of appealing to a broader audience. Beauty, fun and brand awareness are some of the functions that may be associated with a design in addition to the practical elements.

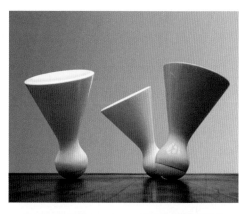

headstand grp*
Understanding the purpose of a product is a fundamental aspect in achieving a successful design. The headstand grp* stool designed by qed* manages to instantly capture the imagination and demand respect through its combined awareness of fun and creativity.

Design:
qed* – Michael Neubauer and Matthias Wieser

Just imagine if it were possible

Aphrodite
The Aphrodite drawer system
manages to defy expectation,
questions user experiences and
captivates the observer by its
unquestionable elegance, grace
and physical beauty.

Design:
Tadao Hoshino –
Edition Ligne Roset

Photography:
Shuya Sato

Left:
Customised parking in Kyoto?
Taking advantage of found
objects or modifying a structure
for personal parking? It is
important to continually be aware
and on the look-out for innovative
ideas, modifications or perhaps
just coincidences that might be
exploited. The parked van and the
structure of the building may
inspire completely unrelated
items at a different scale;
however, the essence of an idea
has been captured and recorded.

To apply sound judgement in the search
for ideas and to consider the obvious are
beneficial and should be acknowledged,
but they do not need to be masters when
searching for ideas. Individuals often do
not have an idea of what they want until
they are presented with the unknown.
It is important for design to explore
uncharted territory. If common sense is
given the opportunity to dictate, thoughts
can be dull, staid and constricted. The
understanding of a logical approach
provides a platform to challenge
convention and enables judgements to
be confronted. Common sense is needed,
but it is also a boundary that should
probably be bypassed in preference for a
sense of adventure during the initial
stages of the unknown.

The initial stages of searching for
ideas should exhibit more freedom than
the latter stages, where they become
refined and considered.

Sense of adventure or common sense:
ambiguous; vague; undefined or obvious
risk; chance; exposure; speculate or defined
opening; opportunity; possibility or safe
freedom; autonomy or boundaries
abstract; impractical; visionary or constraint
naïve; open; unaffected or experience

ere possible > **Common sense is needed** > Explore and have fun!

Photo diary

The photo diary is a valuable device in understanding an environment and capturing detail which may be otherwise missed or forgotten. The recorded image can inspire thought and provide a stimulus for recalling other sensations such as smell, texture and sound.

A constant practice of recording experiences is necessary for providing a valuable impulse into the creative process, but also to provide reference material for unfolding projects or for historical evidence.

The photo diary is useful for recording and understanding a particular experience, such as the problems encountered by a commuter waiting for public transport and then appreciating the issues of the ensuing journey. Empathy can be developed by observing the circumstances individuals have to endure step by step.

Kyoto commuters photo diary
The expectations of commuting can be captured using a photo diary, providing valuable knowledge and background information.

Common sense is needed

New York cab photo diary

A real experience can be recorded using photography and analysed at a convenient point later on. The photographs assist in understanding a particular situation, capturing detail which may have been missed, and aiding the recall of the overall physical and emotional encounter. Comparisons of different journeys or situations can be made to develop an informed impression.

Observing a situation from different perspectives can be recorded successfully using a photo diary. Actual experiences and third-party experiences can provide contrasting information, which may need to be considered equally.

Empathy > Profiles

Understanding a problem

Developing a product requires an understanding of the user to appreciate their position and situation. Everybody is different and everybody has their own agenda for doing things a certain way, which may not be through choice. An affinity with the user needs to be developed so that responses to problems can be suitably tackled.

It is common practice to simulate a situation to gain a better insight to a particular difficulty and to physically appreciate what is going on. It is hard to understand the problems encountered by others unless those wanting to know can confront their real situation effectively. Various methods are possible to relay the experiences of an individual to others and they often involve the use of a prop to prohibit or remove a particular sensation, such as touch or balance.

Appreciation of a sense being removed immediately helps to put the core issues into context and provides a useful reality check. Ignorance of empathy can result in worthless and inappropriate solutions no matter how beautiful the object.

Goggles

The use of scratched or dusty goggles or glasses can give the sensation of poor vision and is useful in developing an empathy with a target audience that may have restricted eyesight.

Many other empathetic situations can be obtained through an innovative use of props.

Common sense is needed

Restrictive props
The removal of a sense can
be emulated using ear
defenders to mask out external
noises. A user's perception
of the environment changes
immediately and empathy can
be experienced with those who
have to work in noise-polluted
areas where important sounds
are not understood.

Empathy > Profiles

Café owners, customers, or passers-by?
It is difficult to understand the status or background of an individual by a simple visual assessment. Frequently individuals are seen out of context and assumptions should be avoided.

Common sense is needed

Assumptions

Making assumptions is a dangerous route to take and should be avoided, or at least approached with much caution. The appearance of a person or the perception of an item can frequently be far from accurate on careful inspection. A third party who is not experienced often makes judgements that are incorrect due to a misunderstanding of the context or situation.

Assumptions are usually wrong and, unfortunately, if given the opportunity to develop, can instigate a series of inappropriate thought patterns and associations. References to stereotypes are damaging and difficult to ignore.

Ideally, objects and individuals need to be considered separately. Does a child buy the toy in the shop or does a relative purchase the item? It is likely to be wrong to assume it is the young child who will pay for the item, but perhaps also incorrect to think that the adult purchases the toy without some element of lobbying from the child? Maybe the adult wants the toy? Relationships between individuals can be very influential and can often result in a person who might be expected to reside in a certain category actually being more orientated to the unexpected.

The Horseman, New York
To appreciate and understand the New York Horseman may be difficult if placed out of context away from the carriages and horses at Grand Army Plaza.

Empathy > Profiles

Collection of items to construct a user profile
Items which might be associated to a specific target audience can be collected and analysed to understand particular traits.

Profiling

Profiling is an important and necessary investigative instrument that provides an insight into the behaviour, habits and routines of targeted individuals. The process is not intended to be intrusive and can be conducted using primary or secondary research methods. The objective is to build an understanding – to probe where necessary gathering detail to formulate patterns which can act as important directional signs.

What are the products that targeted audiences are purchasing? Where, how and why do they use them? These are some of the issues that can be addressed using profiling strategies. To gain a snapshot of attitudes, values and behaviour, simple association methods can be conducted, such as identifying and collecting products affiliated to a particular group.

Exploring and examining collected items can highlight commonalities including attention to detail, quality, or patternation preferences, but can also depict issues such as financial positioning, material usage tendencies and brand awareness.

The intelligence obtained through profiling should be considered in the design process.

How to

It is important to be able to recognise the personal preferences of an individual when it comes to product selection and particularly necessary to identify target audience preferences. What are users buying and what is it that is attracting them? Collecting artefacts, images, materials and other tangible evidence, which are believed to be associated to a particular target group, begins to provide an understanding of what they like, strands of evidence that can inform the design direction. Target audiences are not simply related to age or gender, so profiles may be applicable to a range of individuals who might initially appear to be unrelated.

Images of key products, which the target audience are likely to subscribe to, should be collected and analysed to understand similarities across the range. Interchanging the images, rejecting some and keeping those that are believed to accurately represent the target group enables a visual profile of preference to emerge and understand what might be required in a particular circumstance. When the criteria changes, the images will need to be reviewed. All images should be kept for further profiling activities.

Empathy > Profiles > Themes

Target mapping

To understand the potential of a proposed product or to appreciate what is required, it is necessary to understand the structure of a community or population and to recognise attitudes and beliefs. Critical analysis of research can identify emerging and potential markets and provide directional indicators to inform judgement.

Understanding a market and recognising how an individual or target audience wants to be perceived is attained through the compilation and organisation of a body of research.

The intelligence obtained should be presented in a logical and instantly recognisable manner and, where possible, should avoid the portrayal of complicated statistics, language and imagery. Any information communicated needs to be clear, concise and focused for it to be useful in the comprehension and formulation of targeted proposals.

Harajuka street style
Harajuka street style in Tokyo has been popularised in Japanese trend journals.

Demographics
Demographics are the statistical information that relate to a population or a subsection within a community and includes income, age, gender and ethnicity. Understanding the demographics of a population provides a valuable insight when appraising or identifying an idea.

Target *n*. A person, object, or place selected as the aim of an attack.

Mapping (map something out) *v*. Plan a route or course of action in detail.

Common sense is needed

Forums

A forum provides a chance for those involved in the development of an idea to review the project and engage in constructive criticism. It is also an opportunity to present an idea to a target audience and obtain an indication of probable responses or impressions should it be made more widely available.

The forum needs to be conducted with set aims and objectives, although the process for achieving this may actually appear somewhat informal and adopt a freestyle approach. The process is not an interview, but a discussion to extract positives and negatives, to understand need and possible reason for change. Individuals should be allowed to interact with the proposed item and examine it carefully.

Immediate reactions such as facial expressions, body language and verbal responses, as well as reactions to the idea when placed in context, should be recorded.

Associations attached to the proposed idea should also be identified. Comments which may appear obvious when raised may well have been overlooked or gone unnoticed during previous appraisals and yet might be fundamental to the potential success.

'25' chair
Forum to assess the potential of the '25' chair designed using aluminium foam.

Forum *n*. A meeting or medium for an exchange of views.

Empathy > **Profiles** > Themes

'As the idea grows, more complex and independent shaping gets easier.'

Torbjørn Anderssen, Norway Says, 2007

Inspired selection

Themes are necessary in the development of ideas and need to be refined through the use of constraints as an idea progresses. A theme usually has a relationship to the product being developed although it may appear random or somewhat abstract. The theme may also be a reflection of a current trend and therefore be remote to the functions of the product, but appealing to the target audience.

Mica MP3 player
Torbjørn Anderssen, Andreas Engesvik and Espen Voll of the design group Norway Says designed the MICA MP3 player in 2005. The manufacturer of the MICA MP3 is Asono, Norway. The theme for the design was initially the plug – connecting to information or power. The elegant and fashionable product can be worn in a similar way to a necklace.

Design:
Norway Says

How to

Selecting a theme that has an association to a product being designed is beneficial in steering the thought generation process. Using standard idea generation techniques, such as brainstorming, identify a series of potential themes for the design of a particular product or need. Issues such as who, what and where will provide direction towards a manageable and relevant theme.

Common sense is needed

Giacomo Balla

Giacomo Balla painted *Dynamism of Dog on a Leash* in 1912. The painting captures the movement of the dog's legs as it walks with its owner. The painting is in the Albright-Knox Art Gallery, Buffalo, New York.

'Walker' rocking chair
The 'walker' manages to capture the essence of a traditional rocking chair through the use of numerous legs, which are arranged to depict an imaginary curve. The design, synonymous to a Balla painting, manages to visually emphasise movement and function and in doing so retains a simplistic elegance.

Design:
Oliver Schick

Photography:
Michael Himpel

'In an age of abundance design should be about formalising values and statements. Every product should tell a story that hasn't been told before. Only this way can the process of designing make sense and bring something to our world instead of burden it.'

Eric Morel, Eric Morel Design, 2007

Funghi
The porcelain lamps are alluring, graceful and functional.

Design:
Jaime Hayón, for Metalarte

Photography:
Mauricio Salinas

The Pee Tree urinal
The sophistication challenges conventional approaches through an intuitive understanding of natural requirements.

Design:
© Eric Morel

Adoption

The adoption of a character in the development of an idea can be both fun and rewarding. Careful examination of the key characteristics of animate or inanimate objects can be exaggerated and modified to influence idea progression and impact on an emerging design with great effect.

There doesn't need to be any logic behind the embracing of a character, as outcomes are open to individual interpretation.

Little Crawly Thing
The visual language of the 16 cabriole legs attached to the seat suggests a scurrying bug such as a centipede or millipede.

Design:
Carl Clerkin

Photography:
Justin Pipergen

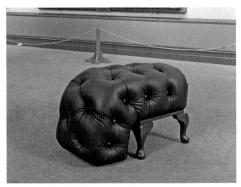

Common sense is needed

Long crawly thing
The use of a repeat form, an understanding of materials and a combination of fun and sophistication, manages to capture an unusual animalistic characteristic in what might otherwise be a mundane piece of furniture.

Design:
Carl Clerkin

Photography:
Philip Sayer

Mnemonics *adj*. Aiding or designed to aid the memory.

Zoomorphic *adj*. Having or representing animal forms.

Themes > Character

'We are all astronauts.'

R. Buckminster Fuller, 1963, Operating Manual for Spaceship Earth, 1963

Literal and lateral

Lateral thinking is a capacity to address conventional thoughts and assumptions related to a particular problem from a different or unorthodox angle. The aim of a creative thinking process is to generate previously unforeseen directions and alternative solutions. The move from a standard thinking method requires imagination and the need to remove preconceptions and bias relating to the problem.

A literal approach to design still requires an imaginative approach, but tends to concentrate on more obvious aspects – a direct interpretation of meaning. The thought process is focused and appears to follow a particular track and clear indicators.

In generating ideas for a design it is worthwhile exploring both aspects of literal and lateral thought patterns and, where possible, to instigate a hybrid approach of the thinking methods.

The process of lateral and literal thinking should not simply be conducted at the initial stages during the emergence of an idea, but continually throughout the development process. The search for improvement needs to be ongoing and subjected to appropriate critical analysis.

A simple item such as the term 'white' can invoke a broad spectrum of responses that include various similes and metaphors. Both similes and metaphors provide opportunity for much manoeuvring of ideas related to the key word. The term 'white' can invoke an exploration of materials, which are physically or mentally cold, but can also be explored in the sense that something is perhaps designed to be simple, meagre or bare.

If literal key words are subjected to sufficient consideration and investigation they can evolve into lateral lines of thought, providing exciting and rewarding possibilities.

Common sense is needed

Chinese whisper

A Chinese whisper refers to the distortion of messages as they are whispered from individual to individual.

Literal *adj*. Taking words in their usual or most basic sense; not figurative.

Lateral *adj*. Of, at, towards, or from the side or sides.

Chinese whisper table
The visual language of the table changes as it moves across the piece.

Design:
Jodie Spindley and Dave Bramston for SaloneSatellite 07

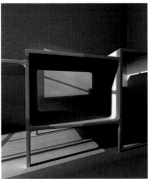

Themes > Character

'The Sony Walkman II entered the market in the late seventies. At the time I was very excited about the device's extremely small size. Not a millimetre was wasted. The standard audio cassette was in effect encased in a thin metal skin containing all the components, such as the drive, audio head and battery. The thing actually felt no larger than the cassette itself. Impossible to outdo, right? I tried anyway! Why enclose the cassette?

Historical influences

To not investigate or consider previous approaches to design, alternative philosophies, constraints and restrictions is probably to miss an opportunity to explore a wealth of exciting ideas that may have been forgotten. Many of these historical influences still have much to offer, although their original context will have changed.

There is a need to question why successful products ceased to exist and perhaps to understand the external pressures that may have been significant in their demise. Fluctuating trends, cultural differences, competition or technological advancements are all significant factors that can instigate a change. It is unlikely that all the components of a product in a historical context are irrelevant to the current consumer, and attention to detail, quality, form and material usage should be considered. Such features are perhaps more important today than they have ever been and therefore, any positive references should be seized.

The development of a contemporary portable music system could undoubtedly gain inspiration from personal stereos, portable record players and transistor radios of previous decades. These ancestor products provide useful references even if the materials, construction methods and target markets have changed, as the fundamental design questions are likely to remain similar.

The amount of ideas, cross-referencing and eclectic knowledge that can be obtained through an exploration of historical approaches is substantial and it is often the case that such products will have something to offer.

How to

There are many sources for gaining historical references. Visits to museums, other relevant exhibitions or places of interest, such as reclaim yards, can provide inspiration. An effective way is to review journals, which reflect a particular period, or style and these may be stored in library vaults. Interviewing people with experience in a particular area is also an example of primary research that can be beneficial. Historical may refer to relatively recent work as well as work produced decades ago.

Common sense is needed

I left it open, showed it, and only created a form-fitting connection with the three mechanical openings. The drive, audio head and battery subsequently hang as a visually separate unit alongside the cassette. Although the resulting 'Museman' had a somewhat larger volume than the Walkman II, the technique of splitting the housing into two separate entities made it appear smaller.'

Jörg Ratzlaff, 2008

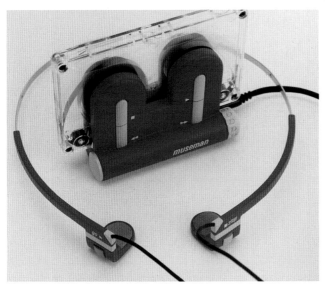

The Museman
The Museman remains an influential piece of industrial design thinking.

Design:
Jörg Ratzlaff for frog design, 1984

Photography:
V Goico

Cultural influences

The term 'cultural' is somewhat ambiguous and is often subjected to different interpretations, which can relate to objects as well as social interaction and behaviour.

It is important to allow different cultural experiences to be encountered and to view different approaches to living with an open and receptive mind.

Ideas can be sourced through an awareness of different cultures and cultural habits. Not to be aware of the way that different cultures interact and respond to situations can be a significant mistake. The anthropologist studies human beings engaging in a broad range of subjects including customs, faith and culture, as well as physical issues and situations. To appreciate cultural influences it is necessary to watch, listen, ask, understand context and comprehend reasoning.

Culture can possibly be defined as a way of life, but it may relate to localised organisations and groups as much as to the customs and practices of individuals from different countries or backgrounds. Influences should be gathered from as many diverse cultural experiences as possible.

Constraints can compound situations where information needs to be gathered. However, irrespective of such pressures, observation of practices, cultures and methods must be given sufficient time to ensure interpretation is accurate and that assumptions are not being made. It may be necessary to interact with a community, organisation or social group for a reasonable period. Interaction will provide opportunity to acknowledge procedures, practices and approaches to a broad array of tasks, some of which may be remote or contrary to familiar approaches and habits. The diverse ways in which issues are addressed in a different cultural environment are very necessary aspects of the design process.

It is important to recognise that an accepted practice in a certain culture may be deemed as an insult or be frowned upon in another. Better understanding of different cultures and practices will almost certainly improve the creativity in design. Observing the ingenuity, inventiveness and imagination of cultures with sparse resources can be as beneficial as observing more developed cultures.

Diversity in culture: Kyoto and Tokyo 2007
The opportunity to become submerged in an unfamiliar culture is an opportunity that should be seized, as every juncture has something different to offer and explore. Even the seemingly familiar is often very different from previous experiences when looked at more closely.

If something is fun it is often addictive and captivating. The natural instinct is to want more and to become submerged in associated activities. When a venture is relegated to the status of a task it can become difficult to be motivated, inspired and to keep the necessary momentum. Consequently, it is all-important to ensure that tasks are not frequently encountered or allowed to evolve into burdens; rather, fun aspects should retain control in the search for ideas and stimulation.

The instigation for thought can come from all directions, and intrigue and curiosity should provide sufficient diversity to explore and engage in virgin territory.

When an activity is informative and responsive it captures the imagination and progress can be made. A 'why not' and 'do what others don't' attitude presents enjoyable and rewarding experiences that usually culminate in a deviation from the anticipated – a place where ideas can flourish.

Left:
The Yellow Sink
The Yellow Sink, part of the beautiful ArtQuitect Edition collection, embraces an elegant theatrical culture with sophistication and functionality. The design explores a harmonious array of visual languages and retains the need to have fun.

Design:
Jaime Hayón for ArtQuitect

Common sense is needed > **Explore and have fun!** > Sensory issues

'I distinguish between Laboratory and Factory.'

Maria Kirk Mikkelsen, 2008

Application

The amount of materials that are available to the designer is fantastic, with global libraries promoting a vast range of exciting possibilities. But it is often through asking questions and exploring fundamental requirements that inspiration and direction can be found.

The basic materials such as wood, metal and plastic cover a huge array of possibilities and when unfamiliar or non-traditional methods are applied to work some of these materials, exciting results can emerge.

Influences for working with materials can be sourced from different disciplines and cultures, which provide stimulating possibilities and sources of inspiration. Materials can and should be challenged and pushed to their limitations; limits that would not normally be considered possible. Investigating a material through simple workshop processes can reveal much about its ability and possible application.

Designing with materials can take different routes. It is possible to conceive an idea and then find an appropriate material to function in a specific role, and it is also feasible to explore a material and then adopt a use for it. It is, of course, also possible to just play with a material and then go and do something completely different. Materials contribute to the soul of a design and their physical and mental beauty should be appreciated, respected and enjoyed.

Maria Kirk Mikkelsen's description of a 'Laboratory' approach refers to a range of creative thinking and investigations, the development of experiences, stories and ideas, whereas the 'Factory' approach, informed by 'Laboratory', is regarded as being more material-based, instinctive and expressional.

Explore and have fun!

'Our inspiration comes from personal experiences or from stories and articles in the media.'

Vlieger & Vandam, 2008

'Design is for me observing the world, analysing meanings of objects and giving visual comments.'

Gijs Bakker, Gijs Bakker Design, 2007

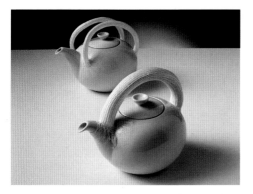

The High-Tech Accent Teapot
The High-Tech Accent Teapot was produced for the German porcelain manufacturer Rosenthal and is made using porcelain and alumina-boriasilica fibres – a material that Gijs Bakker discovered being used within the kilns, being capable of withstanding the melting point of porcelain.

Design:
Gijs Bakker for droog

Guardian Angel bag
The Guardian Angel bags appear to conceal weapons and are a response to the actual and perceived stories relating to crime and antisocial behaviour. The design has been part of New York's Museum of Modern Art's (MoMA) permanent collection since 2006.

Design:
Carolien Vlieger
and Hein van Dam

Foam Rose divider screen
The polyethylene foam design, inspired by traditional lace work and Islamic tiles, was selected in 2005 for the Charlottenborg Spring Exhibition in Copenhagen.

Design:
Maria Kirk Mikkelsen, 2004

'There are plenty of new ideas. It's quite easy to get a new one. But the point is that we should look for ideas which are really useful. Ideas that satisfy a human request, respect ecological aspects and/or make our daily life easier and more joyful.'

Bjørn Blisse, 2007

Enjoy

If something isn't fun it is perhaps necessary to ask why or at least think how it could become more enjoyable.

Designing a product following the same routine and formula each time will soon become monotonous, dull and uninspiring and there is a danger that a creative production line that turns out thoughts without really understanding the problem will ensue. A varied approach, communicating with different people and encountering different experiences, will alleviate any frustration and bring alternative perspectives into play that may not have been considered previously.

When a particular approach seems to have nothing more to offer, a change of course can provide the necessary incentive and inspiration to restart the imagination. Experimentation with mixed or individual components of an idea, that are perhaps closely aligned to personal experiences, provide an opportunity to mentally connect with a design and encounter a positive relationship that has meaning.

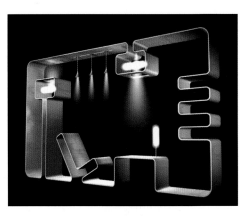

Living in a Box
Design group Transalpin's *Living in a Box* unifies usually disparate items of furniture with a continuous line, creating a physical and fun relationship that is not usually possible. The visual purity of the seat, table, lights, walls, floor and shelving merge as one in an elegant, graceful and personal environment; an environment where restrictive and unsightly umbilical cords have been removed.

Design:
Transalpin Design Group

Photography:
Bjørn Blisse

Explore and have fun!

'Reconfiguring. Giving banal and overlooked objects a new meaning.'

Stuart Haygarth, 2008

Tide Chandelier
The intriguing, curious and seemingly random translucent, clear and transparent plastic components of the 'Tide Chandelier (2004)', deposited by the sea on the beeches of Dungeness, includes broken or distressed everyday artefacts such as combs and spectacles. The previously rejected items cast aside by the sea have been collected and carefully composed into the spectacular chandelier, their collective presence and unsuspecting relationships creating a fascination and elegance that captures the imagination.

Design:
Stuart Haygarth

Materials > **Fun** > Communication

Innovation

Why are things done the way they are? Is it too dangerous to depart from the comfort zone? Exploring and systematically interrogating the various components of a product or the conventional methods of manufacture can conjure up a multitude of potential directions, as well as query the actual purpose of accepted approaches or practices. An audience seldom realises what is required until it is presented, as premature judgements relate only to previous encounters, knowledge, expectations and experiences. When a manner for doing something is scrutinised and called into question it is likely to unleash a myriad of exhilarating proposals, which challenge conservative values and a 'will do' attitude.

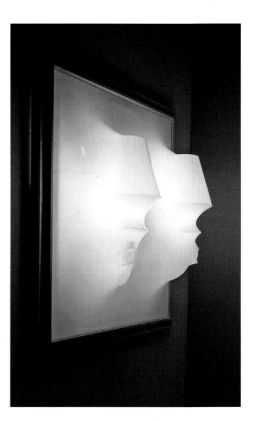

Wall lamp
The innovative approach to lighting challenges convention but retains an acceptable visual language.

Design:
S.M.og Milano. Exhibited at SaloneSatellite 07, Milan

Innovative *adj*. Featuring new methods or original ideas.

Explore and have fun!

Braided wire chandelier
The woven structure of
the chandelier is constructed
from wire, which is usually
hidden away, creating
distinction and individuality
without compromising
lighting performance.

Design
S.M.og Milano. Exhibited at
SaloneSatellite 07, Milan

S.M.og Milano

S.M.og Milano was founded by
Silvio Betterelli and Martina
Grasselli and developed as
an 'ideas factory'. S.M.og Milano
successfully combines
experiences from fashion and
art and design disciplines to
generate innovative, informed
and absorbing designs.

Materials > **Fun** > Communication

'IDEO think of prototyping in three main phases:
inspire: evolve: validate. The inspirational phase is the
right place to try out ideas by making things, to use low-
resolution techniques, and to embrace failure...
Demonstrating the initial configuration of a surgical device
used a marker pen, a film canister and a clothes peg.'

Bill Moggridge, IDEO

Blowtorch
A dirty model of a blowtorch
made from found objects in the
studio including a straw, a can
and a marker pen.

Explore and have fun!

Dirty model

Producing a 'dirty' or 'junk' model is an effective and rewarding process, which assists significantly in understanding the basics of a problem, initial ergonomic issues and subsequently, the fundamental elements of an idea.

Readily available objects become improvised materials, which are generally integrated into the emerging and spontaneous form. The items do not need to be special, rather a simple approximation of what is needed and assembled using available means. The developed ideas can be interchangeable so that various thoughts can be appraised.

There are no particular guidelines in the generation of such a model except that imagination and creativity should be employed, and that outcomes should be understood in an appropriate context. The dirty model is not produced to be beautiful or elegant; it is generated to be informative and provocative.

An understanding of an idea can be conducted expeditiously using screwed-up paper from a phone book or newspaper and attaching the individual parts together to evolve into a potential form. The process informs effectively, although it might not be visually pleasing.

As the development and evaluation of dirty models is instant, it is possible to incorporate perishable elements into the process to understand or represent textures and similar attributes. Anything readily available should be considered to be viable.

How to

The production of a dirty model is a process used by many leading design offices and is effective at achieving instant information.

The development of a dirty model should be quick, gluing or taping found objects together, to generate a rough appreciation of an idea without bias. Aesthetics are dominated by vague approximations.

Dirty models

Materials for dirty models might include: paper clips, hairgrips, paper cups, fizzy drink cans, elastic bands, pens, straws, waste paper, oranges, tape, wire, buttons and scrap card.

Scale

Observing the scale of different environments provides a wealth of potential reference material that can be utilised to consider balance, proportion, composition, texture, materials, detail and relationships. An assortment of visual influences from different backgrounds can be adjusted to formulate comparable scales and influence possible directions.

The surroundings of an object reaffirm physical proportions, but without such references it is often difficult to recognise size and much easier to view things without bias.

Sunday
In 1989, Dietmar Henneka photographed the SUN: SPARC stations designed for Sun Microsystems by frog design. The photograph, titled 'Sunday', featured on the back cover of the July edition of Design magazine and depicts the various SPARC stations surrounded by small model figures, which creates an impression of working and living in a dominant city.

Design:
frog design

frog design

frog design is a 'strategic-creative consultancy' with offices worldwide. Initially founded in 1969 as Esslinger Design by Hartmut Esslinger, the company became frogdesign in the 1980s and then frog design in 2000.

Explore and have fun!

Top:
The Asahi building
The form of the Asahi building and the distinctive 'flame' challenged conventional approaches to scale.

Design:
Philippe Starck, 1989

Bottom:
Changing scales
Details of buildings taken out of context can prompt ideas at different scales.

Fun > Communication > Product language

'Generating ideas in design for me means to enter a trip.
Just give your ideas the right time to speak with you.'

Simone Simonelli, 2008

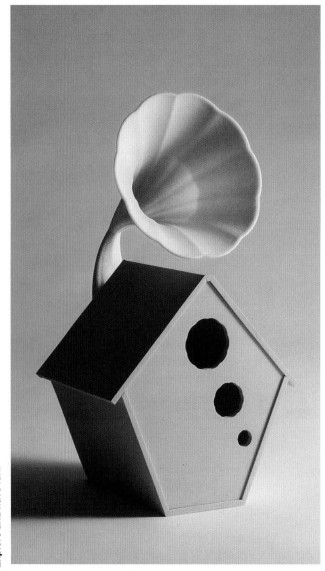

Bird's House
The inspiration for the designer
was a combination of nature and
dreams; the dreaming of new
sounds was initiated during
exposure to a noisy and chaotic
environment.

Design:
Simone Simonelli at Industreal ®
– All rights reserved

Photography:
Ilvio Gallo
www.industreal.it

Explore and have fun!

Form

The architect Louis Sullivan stated that 'Form [ever] Follows Function', a dictum that has been the basis for much discussion ever since. Both 'form' and 'function' are terms that could be further debated as the function of a product is not always what it might initially be perceived to be. A product can be produced with a primary function of simply being beautiful; a function that is probably intrinsic to the form and cannot be judged in isolation from the other. The maxim tends to imply that form is simply a 'skin' dictated to by a predominant function; however, designs often incorporate aesthetic judgement and/or fun elements, which are not necessarily defined by the assumed and incorrect primary function.

A sculptural approach to design can certainly provide the opportunity for form, beauty and elegance to become as important as any perceived fundamental objective.

The Phonofone
The small, but beautifully proportioned Phonophone speaker echoes the form of a gramophone.

Design:
Tristan Zimmermann

Fun > **Communication** > Product language

Alternative thinking

Appreciating the work of inspirational artists provides a valuable introduction to alternative thinking, approaches and execution. A blinkered attitude to all around and the practice of others is not a blueprint for success and will neither introduce nor stimulate different directions for thoughts and ideas.

Disciplines such as sculpture constantly challenge accustomed perceptions of what can be achieved with materials and should be acknowledged and respected.

The Sun, 2006
New York Botanical Garden,
Bronx, New York.

Design:
Dale Chihuly (Artist)
www.chihuly.com

Photography:
Terry Rishel

Explore and have fun!

Peacock Blue Tower, 2001
Garfield Park Conservatory,
Chicago.

Design:
Dale Chihuly (Artist)
www.chihuly.com

Photography:
Terry Rishel

Monarch Window, 1994
Union Station, Tacoma,
Washington.

Design:
Dale Chihuly (Artist)
www.chihuly.com

Photography:
Russell Johnson

Explore and have fun!

Neon Tumbleweeds, 1994
The delicate and flowing
movement of the Neon
Tumbleweeds, created by artist
Dale Chihuly, is reflected in the
artistry, balance and grace of the
Oregon Ballet Theater at the
Portland, 1994 Artquake event.

Design:
Dale Chihuly (Artist)
www.chihuly.com

Photography:
Russell Johnson

Fun > **Communication** > Product language

Appearance

The way a product appears and the manner in which it communicates a visual message are similar to the way an individual appears and the messages they portray. The physical difference between a smile and a stare is slight, but a misunderstanding could have unexpected consequences. A smile is probably the preferred or accepted gesture in almost all situations but, occasionally, an alternative reaction may be fortuitous.

The visual language of a product can be manipulated to emphasise a diverse range of signals that may be consciously or subconsciously recognised by a third party. It is not always necessary to consider the semiology of a product in detail as the message it communicates may simply be a culmination of other considerations, but in some cases the signals portrayed are fundamental to the success and need to be recognised.

Attributes, associated to a product such as form and materials, can be selected to enhance a desired or inherent message. The selections may be basic, but they can be effective communicators if considered carefully. Many products are categorised or stereotyped due to their particular visual language, and yet considering an alternative or unfamiliar language for a product can be refreshing.

----

tp1 phono radio
The design of the tp1 portable/phono radio communicates a functional control and technical understanding.

Design:
Dieter Rams for Braun, 1959

Explore and have fun!

Semiotics *pl. n.* The study of signs and symbols, and their use or interpretation.

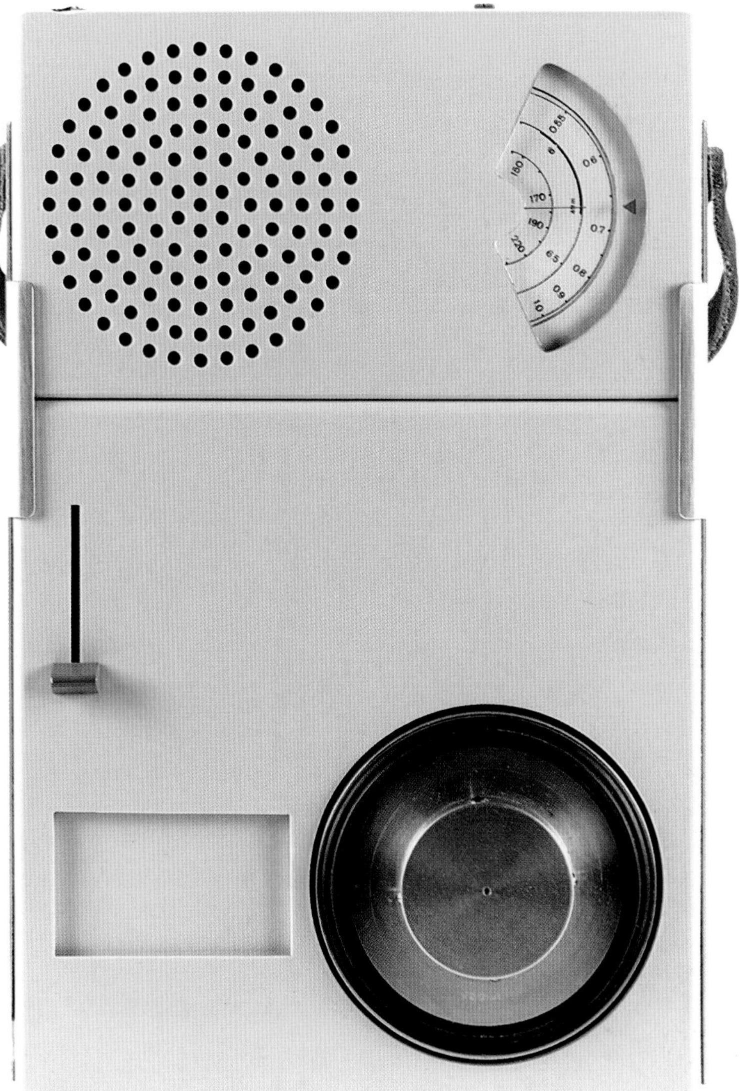

'My intention is to investigate the potential for creating useful new designs by blending together stylistic or structural elements of existing chair types. I see this as a chance to create a 'three-dimensional sketchbook', a set of playful yet thought-provoking designs that, due to the time constraint, are put together with a minimum of analysis.'

Martino Gamper, 2007

Experimentation

What works, what doesn't? Is it possible to ascertain an immediate outcome? Experimenting, investigating, exploring and enquiring allows for ideas to be teased out. Making mistakes, incorrect judgements and questioning is all part of the experimentation strategy. To make a mistake can often be seen as a positive, and an opportunity to reject a particular line of enquiry. A mistake may even enlighten and provide previously unconsidered opportunities.

To experiment is to understand, to reason and to progress. The courage to try something new or unexpected will often result in the opportunity to open up original lines of enquiry and to lead. If designers and artists did not experiment then a certain excitement, intrigue and curiosity factor would be removed.

The designer Martino Gamper collected an eclectic array of abandoned and forgotten chairs for two years and then embarked on 100 days of questioning, understanding and reworking their function and character. The outcome, a collection of 100 chairs, are all individual and each has a story to tell.

Explore and have fun!

Experiment *v*. Try out new things.

Plastic Fantastic
100 chairs in 100 days

Design:
Martino Gamper, 19 July 2006

Ch'Air No 9 chair
100 chairs in 100 days

Design:
Martino Gamper, 19 July 2006

Side Effect chair
100 chairs in 100 days

Design:
Martino Gamper, 24 July 2006

Communication > Product language

Mono Suede
100 chairs in 100 days

Design:
Martino Gamper, 3 March 2005

Sonet Butterfly
100 chairs in 100 days

Design:
Martino Gamper, 25 July 2006

Explore and have fun!

The 'Mono Suede' chair
was the original chair produced
by Martino Gamper in the
100 Chairs 100 Days project.

Black Skirt
100 chairs in 100 days

Design:
Martino Gamper, 27 July 2006

Olympia
100 chairs in 100 days

Design:
Martino Gamper, 2 August 2006

Barbapapa
100 chairs in 100 days

Design:
Martino Gamper, 24 July 2006

Back Seat
100 chairs in 100 days

Design:
Martino Gamper, 13 August 2006

A Basketful
100 chairs in 100 days

Design:
Martino Gamper, 18 August 2006

Tubolare
100 chairs in 100 days

Design:
Martino Gamper, 10 September
2007

Explore and have fun!

'The project suggests a new way to stimulate design thinking, and provokes debate about a number of issues, including value, different types of functionality and what is an important style for certain types of chairs.'

Martino Gamper, 2007

Backside
100 chairs in 100 days

Design:
Martino Gamper, 3 September
2006

Arne Cubista
100 chairs in 100 days

Design:
Martino Gamper, 9 September
2006

Communication > **Product language**

Feel seating system
The Feel seating system has an
emotional attraction.

Design:
Sarit Attias and Amit Axelrod,
for Animi Causa

All of the senses need to be engaged in considering ideas and seeking inspiration from the surrounding environment. It isn't necessary – or perhaps even desired – to replicate all of the aspects of something that provides stimulation, but simply to try and recognise and understand what it is that is creating the interest, capturing the imagination and encouraging the process. The senses are continually at work through conscious and subconscious means and everyday experiences become a creative resource.

The way the senses respond to different stimulations changes depending on external factors and conditions; therefore something might only be of interest in a particular setting or moment in time, or presented in a certain light. The aim is to translate what is being observed or understood through the different senses into a tangible product – a product that might be able to retell or communicate the experience.

It is often difficult to reinterpret an emotion or a primary response due to a context being misconstrued or misunderstood; however, a product that can communicate effectively and stimulate the senses positively is usually desired.

Inhibitions and inexperience should not prevent ideas from being explored and considered, but rather should be a vehicle to enquire and to consider what can be communicated through a design. Subtle differences in interpretation can impact significantly on what can or can't be accomplished with regard to sensory stimulation and overall aesthetic perception.

It is often the case that a situation feels right and although a particular aspect might not be identified, there is something about it that should be explored and examined for possible adaptation or transposition. In such circumstances, the situation is perhaps more instinctive and visceral and such occasions should not be overlooked. The spirit and soul of an idea is perhaps a combination of sensory and instinctive awareness and it is not uncommon for products to adopt life characteristics in their make-up.

Texture

Holding, feeling, touching, caressing and manipulating are activities that provide an understanding of a material or a form, all of which can trigger inspiration for ideas from what might appear to be random objects. The craftsman will often hold a material to feel and sense quality prior to engaging on a particular activity; the way something feels is of the utmost importance. The sensation of touch can be encountered anywhere and at any time and the sudden realisation that something feels good should be recorded. Indicators such as sculptures or banisters that have become polished because generations have touched, felt or enjoyed them might provide an awakening to a possible direction, as may the used form of soap or weathered shells, rocks, wood and pebbles on a beach. Such delicate forms can be held and caressed to appreciate the overall form, but can also further stimulate understanding of textures.

Textures are often incorporated into a design to hide manufacturing defects as well as to enhance the property of a particular object. Seeing through touch on a continual basis will provide a valuable understanding of textures and their significance in the search for ideas. It should be recognised that not all touch is conducted using the hand, and that it relates to the overall body surface.

Right:
Nautilus
The appealing form of the nautilus can inspire direction. The need to touch items of such beauty is almost compulsive and understanding the attraction should be recognised. Objects with appealing contours, textures and traits can be influential in thought development.

Photography:
Keith James, 1993
www.kjamesphotography.com

How to
Constantly be on the look out for textural references through tactile and visual means. Consider changes in scale and how something could be utilised in a different context. Texture is often a very subtle attribute to a product rather than a dominant aspect, but its presence can have a significant impact regarding overall appeal.
    Keep photographic records and annotate images from journals in scrapbooks or notebooks. Interact with products to appreciate their tactile qualities.

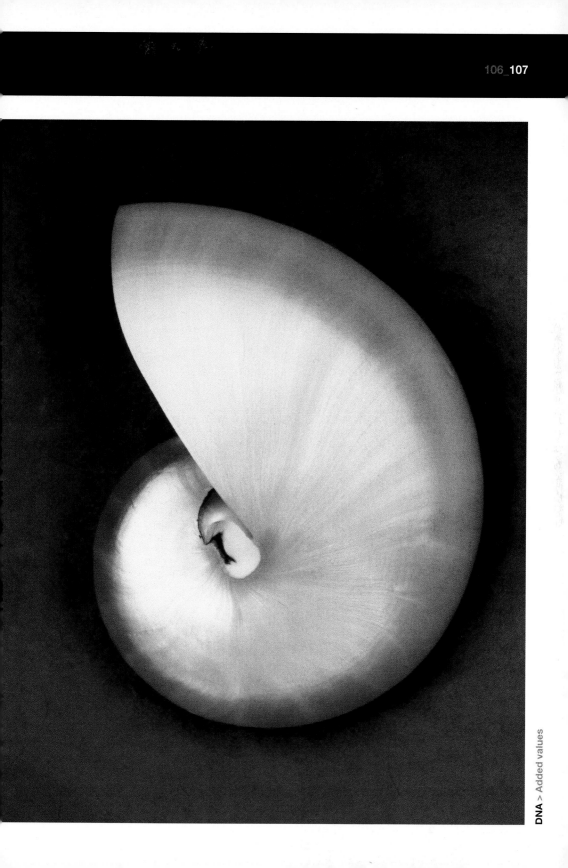

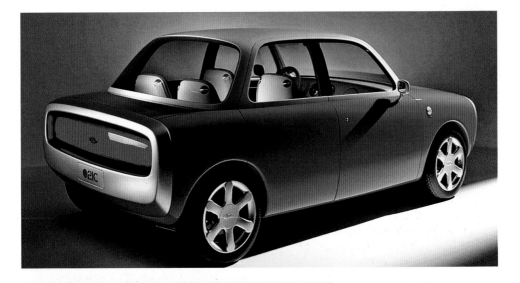

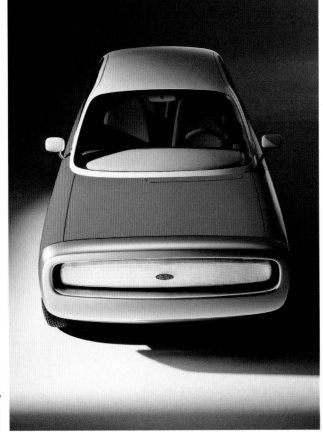

The Ford 021C concept car
The pure and captivating Ford
021C concept car, with its
functional fun aesthetic is aimed
at appealing to young target
audiences. The simple language
is engaging, creating an
atmosphere of innocent
sophistication with a creative
appeal.

Design:
Marc Newson for Ford Motor
Company.
www.marc-newson.com

Photography:
Tom Vack, 1999

Colour

If someone is asked to say what their favourite colour is, the response might be pink. However, this information is probably useless due to the vast range of colours that could be categorised as pink.

Colour is an important component in the design process and if not considered carefully can often be the deciding factor between a product being successful or not – no matter how fantastic the item is. Research has shown that colour is understood faster than most elements, such as (and in particular) form, and so in the split second that an individual makes a selection it is often colour that is informing the decision. Incredibly, it is also often the case that colours are not considered in the initial stages, making an appearance only in the latter phases. The reason is perhaps understandable in the sense that a design idea could be rejected early on simply because of its colour rather than its functionality; but colour should also be regarded as a functional component and not just as an appealing aesthetic.

Colour theorists have often demonstrated that colour can be associated with a range of properties including perceived weight, smell, taste, strength and gender, often due to previous tangential experiences encountered by individuals. The associations are not difficult to comprehend, i.e. dark colours being regarded as 'heavy' and bright colours being considered to 'taste' good. However, pink can be a dark colour or a bright colour: it depends entirely on the actual colour (tone) being presented.

Inspiration for colour selections and combinations are everywhere and it is useful to collect fragments or swatches of colours to clarify what is being considered. Scrapbooks with swatches should be collected continually and specific colour themes, such as the pink example, will soon present an array of possibilities.

Sourced colours can be matched to professional colour palettes to ensure clear communication of a desired colour is being made.

Tribal language

A tribe is usually the term used for a group of individuals with a common ancestor that adhere to accepted habits, procedures and traditions. The tribe is distinguishable from other similar groups through these mannerisms and customs. The agreed standards provide identity and enable them to be understood, recognised and respected for who they are and what they stand for.

Tribes and tribal languages exist amongst products in much the same way that they are present amongst groups of individuals; an aesthetic signature that is unique to a particular approach or set of beliefs forming distinguishable traits. Distinctive characteristics might not be apparent on any initial investigation, as they probably do not relate to an obvious identifier such as form, but rather to an inherited approach or relationship between the items. The history of the products may be identical and so too the influences and target audiences, but this does not mean that the objects are simple facsimiles. The products can be diverse with differing functions, behaviours and performances, but languages used in their initiation will have commonalities.

Observing familiar elements and understanding lineage provides a useful vehicle for the direction and development of ideas as well as an appreciation of recognised constraints.

The generation of ideas and the emergence of a product family can be through an identified philosophy with set aims and objectives, but it is often the case that a particular aesthetic is not fully understood until a broad range of items have been developed allowing a distinctive pattern to be recognised through retrospective appraisal.

Production methods, attention to detail, sculptural appreciation and quality can all contribute to the tribal language of a range of products, even if the materials employed are not uniform. It is often such attributes that define the existence of a particular language rather than appearance alone.

Serene mobile

The Serene mobile phone, designed by Chief Designer David Lewis, was created and launched by Bang & Olufsen in cooperation with Samsung in 2005.

Design:
David Lewis

Beo Center 6

The Beo Center 6, also designed by David Lewis for Bang & Olufsen, was launched in 2006. Attention to detail, finish and aesthetics create a tribal language of quality and sophistication that is evident within the Bang & Olufsen range.

Design:
David Lewis

Smell

It may not seem important to consider smells but, if functioning correctly, smells can be extremely sensitive and capable of triggering memories and recalling specific details.

Smells are useful in the search for ideas and in remembering past situations, but they can also be adept at enhancing or discriminating an idea path through exactly the same mechanisms. As there may not be any physical visual pointers with recalling a particular smell it is possible to receive mixed messages; messages that have the same trigger but recall different events for different individuals.

Is it possible to be put off a product because of the way it smells? The dodgy second-hand car dealer will spray the vinyl seats of a car with preferential scents to hide musty odours or to give an impression of leather, and the baker will ensure that the smell of freshly baked bread is directed at passers-by.

A consumer of a product may be influenced into making a purchase because of a smell that is emitted and the association that accompanies it. It would certainly be unfortunate if a product was to be rejected on the basis of smell, but associations are powerful and should not be overlooked.

Materials that change their physical properties under different conditions will often result in different responses being made by the senses. Smells emanating from a material in familiar settings may well change in unfamiliar environments or climates.

Intense smells
The intense smell of a material in certain surroundings or under particular conditions can trigger emotional and physical responses, which may or may not be beneficial.

While sitting in a train carriage, it is almost possible to smell the history of the materials. Careful consideration should be given to the selection of materials if they are to be subjected to a diverse range of stimuli.

Sounds

How important is a sound? The sound of a door closing or a button being pressed can be an indicator of quality – or at least a perceived quality. Sound associations to a product are important and should be carefully considered. A switch that makes an audible click may be needed in some solutions, but considerations should be given to alternatives. What does the action of switching something on represent? It may mean the start of a rest period for the user or it may be an indication that something is about to occur. Whatever the reason for a particular product, sound quality should appeal to the senses. The sound should not simply be a by-product of circumstance, but rather something that is integral to the user experience.

The integration of personal ring tones to cellphones enables the user to have an enhanced experience and to stamp their own audible preferences. There are numerous products where such experiences could be encountered and could enrich an experience with careful consideration to a note, pitch, tone or melody.

Sounds everywhere
Sounds are everywhere and have an important role to play in design. It is difficult to get away from audible triggers as they can intrude and confront with surprise.

DNA > Added values

'Creativity grows at the intersection of technical considerations, the needs and desires of people, and an aesthetic point of view. We look further than keen problem solving abilities and look for people who are self-inspired, people who are naturally curious about the world. And then we foster that creativity in an environment that allows and rewards risk taking.'

John Edson, Lunar Design president

Something else

The purpose of design must be to improve quality of life in some capacity, and this basic premise applies to whatever is being considered. If something cannot fulfil this fundamental aim then it should probably be rejected at source. In the search for ideas, consideration should always be given to the primary objective, but it is also useful for thought to be applied to the potential of any added values that might be incorporated. The advantage of considering added values is that an initial thought could, through simple or even inadvertent changes, adopt a characteristic or function that is additional to purpose and will either complement an idea or enable it to be considered in a previously unforeseen sphere.

Added values can emerge for aesthetic or functional reasons and rely on the ability to identify and exploit an opportunity.

The Torch 600 light
The beauty and structured simplicity of the design of the Torch 600 light is in many ways overshadowed by the delicate and captivating rays of light, reminiscent of shafts of sunlight, that it emits.

Design:
Finn Kaerulff Clausen
for Contact Design

Left:
Cake plate
Lunar Design's 20th anniversary commemorative plate solves the problem of what to do with the cake and the candle.

Design:
Lunar design

Photography:
Vanessa Jespersen-Wheat

DNA > Added values > Conflicts

'We like to find something fantastic in the mundane, looking at everyday life we try to inject some humour and play.'

Richard Broom, 2008, thorsten van elten

Stamp cups
Stamp cups, designed by Valeria Miglioli and Barnaby Barford for thorsten van elten, 2004, transform unsightly tea/coffee stains into something beautiful.

Design:
Valeria Miglioli and Barnaby Barford for thorsten van elten, 2004

Little Joseph
A simple solution for a candle
holder that combines practicality
and intrigue.

Design:
Maxim Velcovsky qubus
design studio

DNA > **Added values** > Conflicts

Pattern and repeat form

Repeating a single form at a similar or adjusted scale can produce visually complex outcomes from what are essentially simple structures. In nature, fractal structures demonstrate the effectiveness of repeated forms and how an apparently complicated network can be configured.

In a fabricated and artificial domain repeated forms can be seen everywhere, although recognising such structures can be difficult as a visual deconstruction needs to be conducted to identify the duplicated shapes.

The complicated structures of objects, such as chandeliers, can often be broken down to identify simple and basic components. Collectively, the initial impression of such designs can appear inconceivable. Obviously the use of a repeated form is only one aspect of the overall problem to be considered. However, considering the simplistic in the first instance is frequently more beneficial than initially attempting the complex.

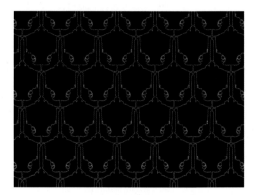

The Ranch Royale wallpaper
The Ranch Royale wallpaper, designed by Maria Kirk Mikkelsen, is part of the 'Make up the wall' collection. The images that are inspired by the Wild West appear to be traditional prints until investigation reveals that they are actually constructed from the repeated forms of skulls or guns!

Design:
Maria Kirk Mikkelsen

Sensory issues

Spiral lights
The repeated forms are used to
formulate the captivating
chandelier.

Design:
Verner Panton, 1969

Product gender

Although it may be preferable to develop items that are non-gender specific to appeal to a broader market, it is often the case that products are positioned for specific audiences. Gender-specific products are carefully researched and aim to consider the conscious and subconscious perceptions of a user. Anthropologists study targeted groups and identify influential pointers and mannerisms to develop cultural awareness that can support the design development process. Patterns of user practice and their interaction with environments can be observed in a variety of ways to help develop understanding. Research needs to be carefully conducted and the target audience understood for the outcomes to be beneficial. Assumptions and personal views need to be set aside and not allowed to bias findings.

Many different influential factors may be considered, which might include fashion sense, personal ornamentation, behaviour patterns, habits, architectural referencing and the relevance of other material possessions. It is unlikely that all observational evidence and intelligence that is gathered will be able to sit together in a single product, but commonality strands running through the reference material may be identifiable for use.

Nokia 7373
The Nokia 7373 phone, part of The L'Amour Collection, challenges conventional approaches to design and embraces a specific gender aesthetic through the considered use of ornamentation and fashion.

Sensory issues

**The aluminium recess chair
collection**
The aluminium recess chair
collection was exhibited at the
SaloneSatellite 07. The chairs use
a simplistic aesthetic to capture
the purity of the pieces. The
removed inner section (the
recess) provides the basis for a
sister chair.

Design:
Dave Bramston
and Neil Housego

Subjective aesthetics

The philosophical area of aesthetics encompasses the fascination of allurement, elegance and attraction of an object with contrasting elements that may be considered to be repugnant, unattractive and somewhat abstract.

Individuals with different attitudes, instincts and reactions have a tendency to favour and engage with a particular aesthetic in preference to another, often for no discernable reason. The subjective nature of aesthetics is difficult to predict as opinions, fashion and appeal fluctuate depending on mood, personal bias, inclinations and experience.

Aesthetic qualities are usually associated to the physical appearance of something and if visual comprehension is difficult to understand, awkward, unnecessarily complicated or proportionally unbalanced, the impression portrayed is often interpreted as being unacceptable.

Aesthetically pleasing elements that are in unison may project a radically different impression if modifications, personalisation or damage occurs. Adjustments during primary investigations can explore the potential of aesthetic quality to gauge a satisfactory outcome.

Aesthetic *adj*. Concerned with beauty or the appreciation of beauty.

Subjective *adj*. Based on or influenced by personal feelings, tastes or opinions.

Added values > **Conflicts** > Emotions

Subtlety

To understand subtlety requires an understanding of judgement and an ability to be critical. An idea can be missed or rejected simply because an element is slightly misrepresented or not communicated effectively.

When an acquaintance or relative has not been seen for some time and then a chance meeting occurs, it is not uncommon for remarks such as 'You look well', 'Have you lost weight?' or 'Haven't you grown?' to be made. Such statements are not planned and are probably not simple pleasantries, but are more likely to be a statement of fact; an instant recognition that something has changed. Unless the separation between the two parties is substantial, the remarks actually refer to what are essentially minor changes in an individual. It might not be possible for the person stating 'you look well' to identify any particular change, but simply to consciously or subconsciously recognise a change. References to height or weight might only be due to a few centimetres or grams, but the change does get noticed.

Subtle differences in an idea or the development of a product can also make the difference between what works well and looks good, and what is readily dismissed. The generation of ideas often results in wildly different propositions; however, simple adjustments to original concepts can result in positive progress and direction. It is not always apparent what has been changed, but changes are often necessary.

Top:
Fat Convertible, 2005
Bottom:
Fat Car, 2001
The works confront 'normal' perceptions using over-exaggerated forms.

Design:
Erwin Wurm

Product respect

The degradation of an adored product can lead to a subconscious neglect and a distancing between user and object. Up until a product receives its initial tarnish (a scratch or a dent) it is respected and cared for; however, when such a disfigurement does occur it is almost relegated to a league of less importance and user focus can become directed at a possible replacement, alternative or a next generation item. The caring attitude can begin to dwindle with the blemished product and the love and respect it may once have been shown gets forgotten. It is, however, not uncommon for products of a decommissioned status to actually become more useable in practical terms.

After the initial shock of the damage is acknowledged and alleviated it can actually begin a sensible existence; an existence in an environment where accidents do occur and are recognised. The scratch or bump usually only impacts on any aesthetic function rather than operational capabilities and if such battle scars are actually understood they can add a unique, distinctive character.

The idea of a product being visually unattractive due to knocks and bumps can be contrasted with its sudden practical status. The concept of scratches, bumps, tears, rips and dents can often be seen as a desired feature and inspiration for originality; as well as an opportunity to personalise.

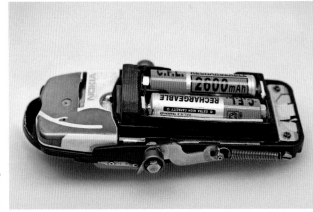

'Custom' or 'hacked' cell phone
With an individual aesthetic and extended existence, Mehmet Erkök used a Nokia 3210 for the experimental work, replacing and altering original components to develop a unique, personalised product.

Design:
Mehmet Erkök

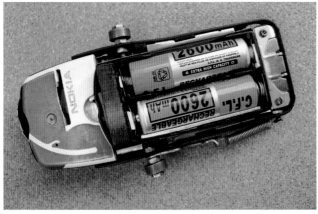

Cellphones
The cellphones of Mehmet Erkök explore rechargeable cells, operational qualities and usability through the use of visible batteries, an ability to 'dress' the phone for specific requirements and an acknowledgement of what Erkök describes as 'stereotypical learning'. The phones have distinctive personalities that demand attention and respect.

Design:
Mehmet Erkök

Emotional response

Happiness, sadness, calm, anger, fear, disgust. Inanimate objects can instigate different emotional responses, to different users, using various inherent qualities.

The response is an instinctive feeling of something that is evident through a verbal or physical bodily movement. A user's emotional response would usually depend on the context of their encounter and intuitive associations. It is possible for an object to arouse, seduce and stimulate beneficial feelings or emotions through appearance and memory. The integrity of these mental triggers can be further affirmed or disbanded through a physical relationship with an object, which may prompt emotional negativity.

The juxtaposition between mental and physical, and positive and negative, experiential emotions is difficult to predict as everything and everyone is unique, but manipulation of an object to assess proactive and negative responses can identify and stimulate exciting ideas.

La femme et la maison.
Ordinary life disturbed
The Maid chair, presented by Nika
Zupanc at SaloneSatellite 07,
explores emotional ergonomics
and questions function. The
emotive aesthetic engages desire
and sensual expression
stimulating imagination and
association. The physical activity
of sitting is challenged by the
emotional experience.

Design:
Nika Zupanc

Conflicts > Emotions

Left:
Portable MP3 unit
The design includes reused
computer speakers, MP3 player,
cardboard box and electrical
cable.

Designer:
Stuart Walker

As a potential idea progresses, the
research that informs the development
becomes more focused and informative.
Primary research strategies are
supported by secondary research
approaches, which aim to reaffirm
thoughts and feelings about
the particular direction of an idea.
An analysis of research methodologies
and ideas needs to be conducted with
ever-increasing rigour to generate
confidence in an emerging proposition.
Focused criticism is required and needs
to be acknowledged and absorbed. In
cases where an idea is beginning to lose
its momentum it needs to be carefully
evaluated to decide if it is to be
terminated. Being able to conclude that
something is not appropriate is a positive
rather than a negative as to peruse
something destined to fail is pointless.

Alternative strategies to assist with
the development of an idea can be
rewarding and can provide opportunities
to view things differently.

Constructive criticism

It is important to be critical, have standards and to apply logical thinking, but not to be destructive in doing so. A critical comment that doesn't offer any direction, any substance or foundation, or is simply a random and speculative remark, is not useful. Such comments should be avoided, as they tend to offer nothing except a negative barrier to creativity. Critical comments are, however, very useful and necessary if structured appropriately and delivered in a suitable context as they often open up previously unconsidered opportunities. It is rewarding to hear positive comments about an idea, but without constructive criticism such remarks are actually unlikely to surface. Everybody has an opinion and if given the stage for too long they will undoubtedly find a reason for inappropriate or ill-considered negativity. Likewise, it is always possible to find someone with a similar view, but useful feedback that can be used should always be sought.

An individual must be critical about his or her design methodologies to understand what is reasonable and challenging and what is not acceptable. It can be difficult to be criticised, but it is necessary to evaluate what is being said and to steer a suitable path.

A passionate and enthusiastic outlook on an idea can develop into a biased opinion, a view that is not beneficial and an approach that should be controlled. Perhaps the acid test for any idea is to ask, 'would you buy it?' A negative or delayed response is possibly enough to warrant another look.

Development of an idea

Self and team analysis

It is imperative that in conducting research and identifying possible ideas or directions that an individual or team understands the problem; a complete problem and not a perceived or isolated problem. Recognition of a problem can come from interaction with a target group but it is possible that even they do not fully understand what is needed or what the problem is. The reason for this is that many activities are conducted automatically without knowing you are doing it, especially when the task becomes familiar. As an observer it is necessary to recognise the forgotten actions conducted by others, and to understand context. Self-analysis of thinking and doing requires a capacity to recognise the unseen and an ability to present accurate findings with evidence.

Bicycle
Certain activities, such as playing a musical instrument or riding a bicycle, can become so natural that it is often difficult to appreciate what is taking place. An observer cannot always rely on a description from the individual concerned as familiar processes are often overlooked or relegated in importance.

Transform

The ability for something to change from the mundane to the extraordinary or for something to be able to evolve and respond to market changes is an exciting and often necessary direction to explore.

The metamorphosis of an object, to transform it into another item, may be an incidental outcome, something that has emerged through accident, but actually functions effectively in either capacity. The permutation can also be initiated by the identification of a constraint or through thinking being directed deliberately towards the need for an adjustable or fluctuating product. Items familiar to a target audience, such as a dresser and divider, or desk and mat, can be coupled together to explore virgin territory and ideas. The identification of a possible marriage between objects – no matter how obscure – will focus thinking and enable innovative thoughts to surface.

The development of an idea should also consider the potential for change that does not engage form but is a result of natural progression or diversification of an audience. The ability for a product to respond to trends or fashion can be observed in the modifications the user makes to a product, but simple changes can also be conducted at the manufacturing stages through the introduction of alternative colours, accessories and functions.

Vase Space
The Vase Space is inspired by American Federal furniture and machined utilising multi-axis CNC technology in collaboration with an American aerospace manufacturer. The flexibility in production allows for modifications and alterations to be made despite the classical form.

Design:
Paul Loebach

Table = Chest
The Table = Chest design
is beautifully simplistic and
captivating. Designed for
Röthlisberger, Switzerland,
the transformation from table
to chest is as elegant as the
individual pieces.

Design:
Design: Shin + Tomoko
Azumi 1995.

Photography:
Thomas Dobbie

The Japanese designers
Shin + Tomoko Azumi formed
Azumi in 1995, producing
exciting, sculptural and pure
designs. In 2005 the designers
began to operate their own
individual design studios with
Shin Azumi operating 'a studio'
and Tomoko Azumi operating
the 'tna design studio'.

The simplicity and surprise
element of the Azumi practice
is captured in the Table = Chest
design and since 2005 the work
of the individual studios has
continued to portray a
simplistic honesty through the
control of functional design and
aesthetic language.

Critical analysis > **Ability to change** > Idea development

Secondary research
Secondary research is an
investigation of already published
findings.

Secondary research

Secondary research is the collection of information that has previously been published in some manner following a primary research approach. The information is not collated using original investigative work, but from understanding the findings of others or from similar experiences.

The differences between primary research and secondary research are important; they both have positive and negative qualities and can be considered in tandem. Whereas primary research provides an opportunity to actually go out and find things first-hand, it is often the case that it is not possible to conduct a wide scale investigation; however, secondary research does allow for a sweep of all published articles and information relating to a particular area to be considered in broader terms.

The somewhat negative side of secondary research strategies is that the information can be presented out of context or can contain inaccuracies and, therefore, it is possible for findings to be unsound or misconstrued. Secondary research strategies may include using reviews of journals, publications, articles and recorded information and these processes can in turn provide sufficient information to instigate a primary research strategy having provided the fundamental leads for specialist enquiry. During the secondary research stages it is necessary to keep a record of what is useful and where it has been sourced.

How to

As secondary research involves looking at previously published work, it can be difficult to absorb a diverse range of information on demand, effectively and efficiently. Although facilities within libraries and research centres exist to aid the execution of secondary research, a good starting point is to be constantly absorbing information by reading journals, reviews, publications and other sources of information on an ongoing basis. It is perhaps unlikely that random reading will specifically relate to a particular problem, but it will provide a valuable platform and background knowledge that will facilitate cross-referencing when required.

Ability to change > **Idea development** > Visual noise

> 'I was at a local bar with a friend, brainstorming on some ideas using napkins. By the time we were getting ready to leave we had a whole stack next to us and wondered: "Wouldn't it be great if there was a way to keep them somehow together?" That thought never left my mind and a few weeks later the Napkinsketchbook was born.'
>
> **Fridolin T. Beisert**, 2008

Starting points

An idea is simply a starting point, a point that may be the initiation of a proposal, but it will need to be interrogated, scrutinised and challenged at every juncture before it is anything more than a notion. If it can survive unscathed and strong it might evolve, but it will need to rely on scores of other positive ideas to support it during a passage to reality. Too often an initial idea is confused with a solution. It is simply a pointer or a glimpse of what might be. The development of an idea is an investigative process, which is continual until sufficient evidence can justify its existence.

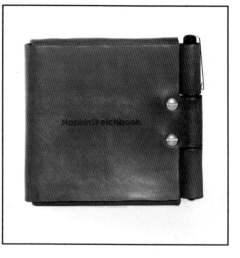

Napkinsketchbook
The Napkinsketchbook is a simple and creative idea that has been conceived through observation and need.

Design:
Fridolin T. Beisert

Photography:
Julia Kopelson

'The Tune 'n Radio is a fm-radio which people have to finish themselves, in order to make the product functional within their own personal perception.'

Wouter Geense Design Studio, 2008

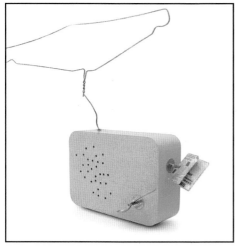

Tune 'n Radio
The radio prototypes are part of the Little Things, Raging Thoughts collection.
www. woutergeense.nl

Design:
Wouter Geense Design Studio, 2005

Ability to change > **Idea development** > Visual noise

Play

Play within design is an important concept as it is through play that social barriers can be brought down, making it possible to engage, understand and develop without inhibitions. Play allows or even dictates that things are kept simple and complications are avoided. If a difficulty arises, play questions and looks for a different rule or approach so that progress can be made and enjoyed. Enquiry within play can be unexpected, random and experimental; questions are constantly asked, answers demanded and 'what if?' thoughts are contemplated until awareness is forthcoming. Tackling ideas through play means that things aren't too serious and thoughts can be thrown away easily or investigated from different perspectives. Play activities allow things to be taken apart, rebuilt and taken apart again so that ideas can be evaluated. An instinctive play approach suppresses obstacles with ease through enjoyment and emotional expression; there is no logic, just feeling along with the inherent desire to discover and make.

Chasing an idea through play becomes enthralling and fascinating; directions that would not normally be unleashed come to the fore and are unable to escape or evade dissection. Reserves and restraints become challenges to overcome, and group activity with different characters and opinions brings different experiences and opportunities.

During play, ideas can be quickly composed and sculpted; things are not resolute and progress can be made through an absorbing indulgence. Play is fresh air, a change from the norm and an opportunity to be exposed to high creativity.

Exploring contrasts using play
The utilisation of simple materials to transmit a basic idea can be effective and direct.

Design development

Developing an idea does not mean jumping between random ideas as problems are presented, but rather exploring the potential and trying to nurture it.

The following terms should be continually explored and considered during the development of a design:

Analyse

Probe

Feel

Instinct

Look

Question

Reflect

Step back

Investigate

Refine

Clarify

Elevate

Improve

Regulate

Rectify

Foster

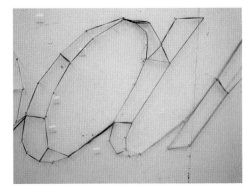

Exploration of ideas and languages using everyday items
Considering alternative approaches to broadly accepted practices of communication allows for unforeseen possibilities to be revealed.

Play is an opportunity to release emotions and should be encouraged.

> 'Less is more.'
>
> Statement attributed to **Ludwig Mies Van Der Rohe.**

Confusing

Noise is generally regarded as being chaotic sound, where confusion is created because of agitated and conflicting messages. Such uncertainty impedes behaviour and a capacity to effectively understand. The notion of visual noise is closely related to audible noise in the sense that when concentrated messages are presented overload occurs. It is not difficult to locate products with an extraordinary amount of futile and nondescript bits betraying an aesthetic, but these credulous products could probably be much improved with an appreciation of sensitivity and less furore.

Visual noise
Numerous instructions, information and characters can have a negative effect on a product rather than actually assisting it.

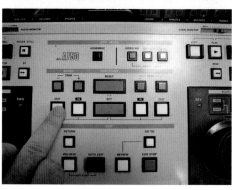

Visual overload
A myriad of messages instigates
confusion and uncertainty. Busy
languages of products are often
functionally detrimental becoming
ornamental rather than useful.

Why not?
In an age where prisoners,
poodles, porches and other
personal belongings get tagged,
the 'tom bunny' rabbit is designed
to be worn around the wrist
of a child or attached to an item
of clothing. Inside the bunny is
a chip which informs parents of
exactly where the child is.

Identifying an exciting idea and being enthusiastic about it is undoubtedly a good thing, but it is also possible to become so enthralled by the momentum of an idea that basic elements are overlooked. Is the design actually that prudent?

Key questions that should be considered when thinking about an idea are:

Is it realistic functionally?

Is it realistic practically?

Is it realistic logistically?

Is it realistic morally?

Is it realistic ethically?

Is it realistic to produce?

Is it realistic to market?

A rethink regarding any problem areas does not necessarily mean a complete redesign, and minor alterations could have significant benefits without being too detrimental to the overall result. The ideas stage is a continuous period of evaluation and progression, although it may become less obvious that changes are occurring as the design evolves.

Product experience

Identifying an idea and developing it is by no means the end of the story. A product needs to be much more than a physical commodity. A product should engage the user, appealing emotionally and intimately to ensure that interaction is positive. A product needs to connect in a manner that is acceptable and personal; the consumer wants more than a tangible thing – he or she requires exposure to an experience, an experience that aligns with his or her own beliefs, standards and aspirations. It is no longer difficult to find products that are comparative regarding physical beauty or function; the distinguishing difference is providing a beneficial experience and making a unique impression.

The experience should not be contemplated after other development matters have ensued, but should be considered at the outset – it is an intrinsic and fundamental issue. A brand experience can always be enhanced further down the line, but its foundations should be prevalent at the initiation of an idea.

Opportunities to fascinate and captivate an audience on an apparently individual level are significant and are more aligned to nurture than manufacture. Every associated aspect to a product needs to be carefully evaluated and understood.

Geek Squad

The Geek Squad, formed in the USA in 1994, has managed to remove the frustration and anguish associated with problems with computers through an innovative approach synonymous to an FBI agent. The Geek Squad agents that are dispatched to solve consumer difficulties have the appearance of a special agent and the computer know-how of a geek. The combination manages to convert perceived obstacles into a rewarding experience. The ability to recognise such issues and manoeuvre them into positives enhances the brand.

Brand *n*. A type of product manufactured by a company under a particular name.

Experience *n*. An event or activity, which leaves a lasting impression.

Experiences > Responsibility

Brand experience

The experience of a brand is influenced through physical, mental and sensory encounters. If an experience is perceived as being contradictory, incoherent or irregular then a unified message is not being communicated effectively and the response can be damaging. Everything needs to be considered carefully and thoroughly to formulate an impressionable dialogue that has meaning and consistency. Consideration and appreciation of the brand experience should be understood from the outset to influence idea direction, formulate desirable objectives and recognise important constraints or themes.

It is as necessary to have empathy with a brand and appreciate what it stands for and why, as much as it is to having an understanding of a target audience and really comprehend what they want. Although a brand experience must work on a personal level it should also be functional on all other platforms where it will be encountered. An evolved reputation of a brand, positive or negative, will almost certainly impact on the individual consumer; attention must be focussed on everything associated with the brand if understanding is to be enhanced as a readily formed impression can be difficult to overturn if incorrect.

Without thought

In the previous year to the launch of the Muji CD player, Naoto Fukasawa had organised the 'Without Thought' workshop that recognised that individuals were interacting with objects and finding solutions to problems unconsciously. The understanding of these inspirational acts provides the basis for innovative and exciting ideas within design.

Blue sky or reality?

Muji CD player

Muji is synonymous with purity and efficiency. The no-logo brand represents simplicity in all areas, including packaging, production and presentation, which enhances both quality and experience.

Design:
Naoto Fukasawa

Sustainability

The maintenance and ability to repair products effectively and efficiently without burden is a necessary factor that needs to be considered on a broader scale. Basic everyday products can be designed using simple components or parts that would normally be discarded after an initial use. The utilisation of such existing features enables a product to almost inherit an extended existence as the various components can be readily replaced or corrected without any significant compromise. There are various interpretations of sustainability; however, when considering ideas the fundamental objective needs embracing.

Lather lamp
The design uses liquid soap bottles, steel rod and cast concrete. The honesty of the design has an appeal and elegance that many fail to capture.

Design:
Stuart Walker

Blue sky or reality?

Wire lamp
The beautifully simplistic light uses mild steel rod, cast concrete and off-the-shelf electrical parts. The design is something that can easily be maintained and repaired by the user.

Design:
Stuart Walker

Packaging

The packaging of a product is an area that needs to be considered with ever-increasing care, attention and understanding, but it does not need to be a compromise.

Packaging should not be an afterthought, but rather something that is subjected to rigorous investigation to question what is actually needed. Why package something that is already packaged? A strange question? Packaging is not simply assigned to plastic bags and polystyrene, it is anything that surrounds something else, a skin securing and often protecting more vulnerable items.

It is not unfamiliar for packaging to be a physical component of a product, something that is not discarded, but rather embraced and which adds value. Natural materials are often assumed to be preferential to synthetic materials, although creative thinking will reveal exciting opportunities that are not harmful to the environment and can actually enhance an idea.

The need to consider packaging carefully has become an influential design constraint in the generation of ideas. Innovation has to be explored and audiences are becoming appreciative of efforts to reduce detrimental effects caused by some packaging.

The notion of reuse is no longer a desire anymore but more a necessity, a necessity that is creating a wealth of ideas. Inspiration for packaging-related ideas are everywhere and particularly in regions where materials are limited and where there is an increased number of design constraints.

What does it say about an individual or a company if there is no consideration to environmental impact when designing or purchasing a product? Target audiences are becoming increasingly aware of social responsibilities and associations.

Package *n.* An object or group of objects wrapped in paper or packed in a box.

Skin *n.* The thin layer of tissue forming the natural outer covering of the body of a person or animal.

Blue sky or reality?

**Ecolo – set of four flower
vases in PP with display box**
The plastic bottles are used
as vases to hold flowers, rather
than being discarded. The
apparent contrast of the flowers
and detergent bottles becomes
insignificant when considered
and placed in context.

Design:
Enzo Mari, 1995
Alessi S.p.a., Crusinallo, Italy

Experiences > **Responsibility** > Projects

Project 1:
Fit in the box

Identify the essential items that are required for a short vacation and then pack as many items as possible into a box that is no larger than a 500g margarine container. Items should not be repackaged or adjusted to fit into the container and so you will need to think carefully as to what is absolutely necessary. In situations where desired items can't be used, innovation and improvisation will be needed to identify something that will do the job instead.

It should be possible to place more than 50 items in the container, but no items can be repeated. Avoid items that you would probably find in a hotel room. When all the items have been collected the lid for the container must be firmly replaced.

Having achieved the initial 50 items remove 25 items, keeping only the essential things left in the container.

Project 2:
Improvisation

Select an innocuous item and consider the different ways that it could be utilised as a particular product.

For example:

A marker pen could be considered as a phone.

The lid of the marker phone could be a detachable speaker.

The marker phone could be held in front of the mouth.

The marker phone could be used to write text messages.

The lid of the marker phone could be turned back and forth to dial.

The cylindrical form of the marker may contain a battery.

Either end of the marker phone might be a speaker.

The marker phone can easily fit in a shirt pocket.

The marker phone could be held like a microphone to speak.

Project 3:
Curious actions

Observe the mannerisms of individuals as they walk towards an entrance to a building. There is often a 'preparation zone' prior to entering a building where people start to physically and mentally prepare themselves for a transition. Mannerisms may include brushing their hair, adjusting their shirt or coat, or perhaps scratching themselves (somewhere). It may also include changing spectacles, applying make-up or simply discarding a coffee cup in a peculiar fashion. There are numerous curious actions that individuals do and observing a flow of people will highlight many of these often unnoticed and unscheduled characteristics.

Observing a scene after a mass of people has passed will also give indications of certain habits. Pathways emerge from shortcuts that have been taken, rubbish bins are piled precariously full and clusters of cigarette ends can be seen in adjacent areas to the main thoroughfare. All of the curious action indicators can provide valuable inspiration for design.

Project 4:
The mall

Making an assumption about an individual and associating a person to a certain stereotype is usually a mistake. Watch individuals as they select items within a supermarket or shopping mall and observe the products that they are placing into their trolley and taking to the checkout. The items that are being selected may be very different to what might be expected. Try to consider why this might be.

Project 5:
The journey

Taking a journey in a taxi, on the
underground or on a bus can provide
an insight into the difficulties that
commuters encounter on a daily basis.
Problems with luggage, communication,
comfort and close proximity to other
travellers can influence perceptions of
an experience. Record a journey using a
camera to highlight issues that may need to
be addressed. The journey should be
conducted several times and at different
points of the day to appreciate the
bigger picture.

Project 6:
Number 11

Identifying a problem and conducting
a brainstorming session releases
interesting and exciting ideas; however,
the initial ideas, which can sometimes
prove to be the most rewarding, are too
often the most obvious. It is not until
there is a struggle to set an idea free
that really interesting possibilities
begin to appear and there is a pull on
mental resources.

A brainstorming session to identify
the different ways that people remember
things might initially include suggestions
such as writing notes on their hand,
putting a knot in a handkerchief or
perhaps turning their watch upside
down. Exploring this line of investigation
further will lead to ideas that instantly
excite and enthuse. Consider further
the different ways that individuals use to
remember things and select the 11th
suggestion for development.

Project 7:
Orange 100

Use found swatches to identify 100 different tones of orange.

Project 8:
Hybrids and scale

Find different images of a family of products and photocopy them at different scales to produce paper-based reference materials. Using the images, cut out key components and place them next to interesting features from other products. The manipulation and apparent merging of the different images can be captured effectively using the black-and-white copier again. The images produced will appear unusual and somewhat disjointed, but working on the copies in black-and-white media will allow the disfiguration to become less noticeable and potential pointers for ideas to be evaluated. Using this simple approach, produce a range of cameras that incorporate aspects taken from other analogous products.

Project 9:
In the post

The average letterbox is approximately 300mm x 40mm and there is a tendency for individuals to order products from catalogues that can't be delivered when they are not at home. Most items that are delivered through a standard letterbox tend to be flat, thin and short; however, it is possible to post more complicated shapes with a bit of thought and ingenuity.

Without posting individual components or compromising a design to the extent that it is not practical, design a single piece of furniture that incorporates a lamp, chair and a table so that it can be posted through the letterbox! It may be easier to begin with card models to identify the different forms that go through a letterbox and then develop the item from this foundation.

Project 10:
Roadside beauty

When a tyre needs changing on a vehicle it is usually during bad weather conditions and poor light. There is never a good time for a tyre change. The process involves the use of difficult-to-access tools, is dangerous, dirty and unpleasant. Design a roadside assistance kit for changing a tyre, which will be produced by a leading skin care company who wants to focus on care for your hands, nails and hygiene.

Consideration should be given to the priorities of the product, but also the emotional requirements of the user. The stigma of grease and grime, along with the hassle and bother of changing a tyre, needs to be considered as an opportunity to refresh and cleanse.

Analogous products might include: dressing tables; manicure sets and beauty salon workstations.

Project 11:
Conker collecting kit

Understanding the needs of others is a necessary feature within the overall design process. Design a non-gender specific conker collecting kit for children aged ten years old. What does the ten-year-old child need for collecting conkers and why is the process important to them? Where will the conker collection take place and what dangers would they need to consider?

Things that the children may want in their conker collecting kit include:

A box to stand on to look out for angry farmers.

A sign to warn passers-by of conker collecting in progress.

Some cones to section off an area.

A collection of tools to obtain conkers.

A container for carrying their hoard.

Steps to reach branches.

Conker collecting protective uniform.

A gang identification badge.

Large gloves to deflect falling conkers.

Conker shell mallets.

'Do not cross line' conker collecting tape.

A method of tagging a tree to let others know they were first.

Camouflage netting to hide equipment.

Compass, map and notebook.

It is unlikely that all the ideas could be used in a single solution and therefore priorities would need to be identified.

Project 12:
Dirty models

Dirty models provide a basic understanding of an idea and can be constructed easily from found material, providing that they have an underlying affinity with the proposal. The important aspect of a dirty model is that they are effective and efficient and so if realisation is too time-consuming it is probably not beneficial to the overall process.

Using found objects that can be sourced readily, produce simple representations of the following items:

A laptop computer.

A cellphone.

A portable TV.

A welding mask.

A tape player.

Project 13:
Analogous uses

Select an everyday item and think of
as many ways as possible that it could be
used in addition to its recognised purpose.
It will be easier if an object is selected
that can be held.

For example a book can be used to:

Read

Fan yourself

Prop up a wobbly table

Create shade

Cuddle and keep warm

Throw at something else

Support other books on a shelf

Keep something held down

Press flowers

Step on

Have an excuse to meet someone

Adjust a projector

Hold a door open

Have as a tray

Hold something hot

Swat a fly

Increase arm length

Give as a present

Push pins in

Make a telescope

Hide something

Hold memories

Start a fire

Dig a hole

Protect from danger

Write notes on

Sit on

Hide suspicion

Protect from rain

Scrape with

Shout louder!

Put drinks on

Stifle sound

Prevent smacks

Hold a secret

Amplify sound

Hit a ball with

Make a goal post

Shield with

Put cake on

Insulate something

Kneel on

Flatten something

Prop a window open

Brush things with

Throw for the dog

Put your head on

Hammer with

Cut on

Mix paint with

Project 14:
Sitting comfortably?

Observe and catalogue the different ways that individuals really interact with a standard chair. Along with the different ways of sitting, identify the other uses that a chair is unexpectedly subjected to. Use photographs to accurately record the findings and collate the information in a notebook with limited annotation.

Project 15:
Supporting structures

Identify ten different objects that are one metre in height or items that can be reduced to the specified size. Use the various objects to support a table with a dimension 600mm x 1200mm or similar.

Project 16:
Two blocks of timber

Using two blocks of wood, each having a dimension of approximately 300mm x 25mm x 25mm, identify as many uses as possible. The separate pieces may be joined to create a larger piece or remain as individual items. Additional parts can be attached to the wood, but this should be kept to an absolute minimum and avoided wherever possible.

Project 17:
20 buckets

A bucket is a very versatile object that is normally purchased to carry things in. However, the bucket can be used to do much more, but is seldom purchased for such reasons. Identify 20 ways that a bucket could be used, which are not associated to carrying. Avoid additional components although material can be removed from the bucket if necessary.

Project 18:
30 seconds

Develop a device that can accurately measure a 30, 45 and 60 second period. The design must be innovative and should be constructed from found objects that are not usually associated to the measure of time.

Project 19:
Sushi lunch

Design a lunch container for the under-seven that allows them to eat a form of sushi at school. The sushi is expected to be child friendly, consisting of parcels of rice and fish or chicken, and is aimed at introducing more experimentation within a child's diet.

Project 20:
Cup of tea

Making a cup of tea is regarded as a simple task and may be defined in the following way:

Add hot water to tea bag.

Remove tea bag.

Add milk/sugar.

Drink.

The above statements may leave an individual, not familiar with the process of making a cup of tea, thinking that it all takes a few seconds. In fact the statements miss out a lot of the detail and this is often because a process has become so automatic that an individual doesn't even recognise what is taking place.

Carefully identify all the stages necessary in the process of making a cup of tea with milk and two sugars.

Having identified the stages, make a cup of tea and record the stages carefully with photography that will also capture the time of the shot.

On evaluating all the information it is likely that the process of making the drink takes considerably longer than anticipated.

Project 21:
Folding wall

Card engineering, such as pop-up books, are incredibly innovative and utilise material effectively and efficiently. The pop-up items are often well considered, but are also often representations of a form rather than an accurate portrayal. Observing the techniques employed by card engineers, design a fold-out working environment that incorporates a desk, light and shelving system for children aged seven to nine years old. The complete design should be able to fold flat against a wall when not in use and may have a secondary function such as a pin board or gallery wall.

Consideration will need to be given to strength and weight of materials, as well as an innovative use of folds and supports. As the design is for a young target market, it is especially imperative that there are no finger traps.

Blue sky or reality?

Project 22:
Park game

Identify a game that can be played in a park or on a beach. The game might be soccer, softball or cricket, it doesn't matter what is selected. Having decided on a place to play the game and what to play you are allowed only one piece of specialist equipment i.e. a football; everything else has to be sourced at the location. A bicycle might become a marker on the pitch, or a bag might become a goal post or cricket wickets. Using your imagination you should aim to replicate as many facets of the real game through improvisation. An improvised substitutes bench, first aid kit, or advertising board may all be considered to bring the game alive and provide an experience, which is not often encountered. Think about ways that the various teams can be identified and innovative approaches to timing the length of the game. The use of improvisation will provide a wealth of opportunities to improve the quality of the game.

Project 23:
Showroom walk

A short walk around the workplace, using your senses, will reveal a host of ideas that often go unnoticed in everyday activity. Evidence can be seen everywhere where individuals have improvised. For example:

A cup holding pens on a desk.

Cardboard placed under a door to keep it open.

A bicycle locked to railings.

A chair used as a step to reach something on a cupboard.

Taking a 20-minute walk around the working environment identify as many innovative uses of items as possible. It should be possible to identify at least 50 such situations in the allocated time. Each of the ideas that are recorded should be evaluated and considered. Is there a need for something, which isn't currently available?

Recall?

To recall something to memory is usually possible, but the detail will not be present without a suitable trigger. A song, a memory or an idea requires inspiration and reference material that can be developed and enhanced if something is to become real.

Singing on a stage with no audience or backing band is as difficult as generating an idea successfully without an appropriate physical and mental support structure.

Collect as much reference material as possible, but know what to use, when and how.

Think of a song and now sing it out loud.
It is almost impossible to do except
for a few lines or maybe some of the chorus.
When there is accompanying music it is a
little bit easier, but listen to the enthusiastic
sounds emanating from an audience at
a concert and you will soon realise that
even with professional acoustic support
it can take a long time to actually hear an
accurate rendition.

The analogy is much the same during
the design process in the sense that it is
often possible to see things in the mind,
but quite a different thing to try and
effectively communicate it. There is a need
to be surrounded by visual stimulation,
images that can assist and prompt thinking
even if they are not directly related.
To be creative without any visual input to
stimulate is not impossible, but almost
certainly more difficult. The hoarding of
objects to rouse and encourage thinking
is a natural characteristic of the designer.
It is equally important to get out of the
studio environment and get involved,
experience things and communicate with
others; to see what is actually going on.
There should never be a situation where
the design process becomes stagnant or
uninteresting and if such times do
occur, there is a need to consider things
from an alternative perspective and to
see what emerges.

Isolation in the design process may
be needed to think for a short time, but
questions should be looked at in unison
rather than a single individual looking
to go it alone. Almost without exception
the design process is a team effort
even if there is a recognised maestro
steering the process.

The research work for *Idea Searching*
did not start when the publication was
conceived, as this was only an identification
of a collection of experiences to be drawn
together. Unknowingly, the research began
decades before on multiple levels and by
many individuals.

'Always look and listen, and do it again.'

Aesthetics
Fundamental principles connected to emotional perceptions and understanding of beauty, judgement, and awareness.

Analogous
A resemblance or relationship between different things. An analogous product is when something seemingly unrelated has a comparable feature to that which is being considered.

Anthropologist
Anthropologists have an important role within the design process as they observe behaviour, mannerisms, attitudes and other attributes of individuals, societies and cultures, providing key information to consider.

Artistic licence
Terminology that usually refers to the generation of a sketch or similar in a two-dimensional format that is not accurate or representative of what is actually being proposed. Artistic licence is often inadvertently used when an idea is not clearly understood or considered. To avoid artistic licence, the generation of simple sketch models or maquettes, in conjunction with two-dimensional sketching, can be used to gain better understanding of a proposal.

Bigger picture
To take a look at something as a whole and its possible outcomes, implications, contexts or consequences, rather than to focus on a single aspect.

Blueprint
A blueprint refers to an original plan.

Brainstorming
A brainstorming session is often regarded as the initial stages of idea generation although this may occur much earlier and can also be an ongoing process. A brainstorming session usually involves a group of individuals responding verbally to a keyword to generate possible ideas. All ideas within a brainstorming session should be recorded.

Catalyst
A catalyst is something that can hasten a process and enable outcomes to occur sooner. A verbal or visual catalyst is something that can be utilised to precipitate ideas and thinking. Catalysts are an important aspect of generating ideas effectively and efficiently.

Ceremony
A ceremony is regarded as an undertaking that follows a prescribed path or format usually due to tradition or religious beliefs. Ceremonies are also frequently adhered to as a way of communicating professionalism and enhancing user experience in a somewhat theatrical manner.

Chiaroscuro
This Italian term refers to light and dark. Chiaroscuro emerged in Renaissance paintings and drawings where there were strong contrasts in light and dark. The approach to using conflicting contrasts of light and dark is now evident in a broad range of creative disciplines.

Chinese whispers
A phrase usually used to describe the miscommunication of verbal information from one individual to another. As a message is passed along its meaning or understanding can become altered or misunderstood.

Comfort zone

The comfort zone is effectively a state of mind, which prevents individuals from experiencing the unknown. Such individuals tend to be less anxious in familiar surroundings. Exploring beyond a comfort zone may be to engage in a risk, but it is necessary to discover and gain original experiences.

Deconstruction

Investigating existing products by dismantling them and conducting an analysis of the various components.

Degradation

The wearing down or physical deterioration of a product.

Demographics

The statistical information available that details specific attributes of a society including births, death, age and wealth. Demographic information can be used to gain an insight into and understanding of a society.

Eclectic

A broad range of styles, ideas or similar, which can be brought together to inform direction and understanding.

Empathy

Understanding the position of others and seeing things from their point of view. It is important to understand a person's feelings and the context that has developed their particular outlook.

Facsimile

An identical copy of something.

Forum

An assembly of individuals to assess the potential of an idea and to exchange thoughts. A forum may include selected members of a particular target group to gain valuable feedback.

Fractal

A component part of a complete form or figure that manages to retain the same fundamental structure despite being of a different scale.

Function

The function of a product is often identified as the actual physical function, but can also relate to many other areas including emotional or aesthetic function.

Haptic

Relating to sense of touch.

Inanimate

An object that is not alive or doesn't portray any evidence of living.

Info dump

A forum to discuss and present sourced artefacts and references, which may or may not be significant in the development of a product. The information collected is used to prompt ideas and to allow others to gain an understanding of identified reference areas.

Inherent

Something that is an integral attribute from within or part of the make-up.

Logistics

The comprehensive organisation of a complicated task to ensure that everything is addressed effectively and efficiently. Understanding the logistics and the manner in which things should be conducted is productive and economical.

Maquette

The term maquette refers to a scale model that is produced to assist in the physical development of an idea. Other terms may include sketch model or bozzetto.

Mental baggage

Preconceived ideas of things, which prevent the development of original thought. Mental baggage can be a barrier to development, but can be overcome through the use of alternative approaches.

Metamorphosis

The transition of something from one state to a different state.

Mnemonic

The development and understanding of how certain imagery, patterns and stories can be structured and utilised to assist the memory. There are many different mnemonic thoughts that individuals use to trigger memories.

Panoramic

A panoramic view is an uninterrupted view of something that captures an entire visual field.

Photo diary

A photo diary is usually a detailed photographic recording of a particular event or situation aimed at highlighting positives and negatives. The contents of a photo diary enable the analysis and understanding of something to be conducted with a certain amount of empathy.

Primary research

Primary research is the gathering of research from first-hand experience and usually requires a 'go out and do' approach. Types of primary research might include questionnaires, interviews or forums with a target audience. Approaches might also require the need to explore current markets and gain appreciation of current practices.

Profiles

Profiles or user profiles usually require the gathering of artefacts or images that are considered or known to be relevant to a particular target group. Understanding the products that groups already associate with provides an insight into what might be developed.

Secondary research

Secondary research can work in conjunction with primary research, but differs in the sense that it is the gathering of information that has already been published by a third party.

Semiology

The analysis of visual languages to determine an understanding or meaning.

Shadowing

A process where the activity of another is better understood by joining them for a period of time to appreciate the situation first hand. Shadowing is a useful form of primary research that can provide detailed understanding that might not be understood otherwise. Shadowing provides a taste of what is occurring and possible directions to explore.

Splicing
The joining together of two or more parts to form a whole. The splicing of images is frequently executed in activities such as montage.

Stereotype
A perception of somebody fitting a particular group or criteria that is often shown to be an incorrect understanding when further investigations are made.

Subjective
Refers to an opinion, often without any logical rationale, that is based on personal understanding, belief or taste.

Swatches
A small sample of something, often fabric or paper, which can be collected and tested or assessed prior to any further commitment.

Tags
Identifiers, labels or signatures that can be personal or generic. An individual may tag an item to be different or may use a tag to be identified with a certain group.

Tangible
A physically existing item as apposed to an imaginary item or thought.

Target mapping
The identification of a particular audience and the subsequent understanding of issues that relate to the emergence of an idea relevant to the group.

Three-dimensional sketching
The practice of generating ideas effectively and efficiently by using found or sourced three-dimensional components. Physical ideas and configurations can be assessed, considered and changed easily in a similar way to sketching in two dimensions.

Thumbnail
A simplistic, efficient outline of an idea in a sketch form.

Triggers
Artefacts, images, terminology or something that appeals to the senses, which can prompt an idea or thought.

Visceral
Connecting with profound emotions and feeling rather than reason, judgement or comprehension.

Visual noise
Visual confusion of messages or understanding of something due to an overload of information or physical details.

Visualstorming
An idea development process similar to brainstorming, but utilising simplistic visual imagery to communicate a thought or association.

Zoomorphic
Term used to describe something that has a form, which resembles an animal characteristic in a particular way.

Bibliography

Aldersey-Williams, H.
King and Miranda: The Poetry of the Machine
(Blueprint monographs)
Fourth Estate (1991)

Antonelli, P.
Humble Masterpieces: 100 Everyday Marvels of Design
Thames & Hudson Ltd (2006)

Antonelli, P.
Mutant Materials in Contemporary Design
Museum of Modern Art (1995)

Bakker, G. and Ramekers, R.
Droog Design – Spirit of the Nineties
010 Uitgeverij (1998)

Benyus, J.M.
Biomimicry
William Morrow (1997)

Bloemendaal, L.
Humanual
Uitgeverij BIS (Book Industry Services),
Amsterdam (2002)

Börnsen- Holtmann, N.
Italian Design
Benedikt Taschen (1994)

Brownell, B.
Transmaterial
Princeton Architectural Press (2006)

Buckminster Fuller, R.
Operating Manual for Spaceship Earth
Southern Illinois University Press (1969)

Coates, N.
Guide to Ecstacity
Laurence King Publishing (2003)

Dempsey, A.
Styles, Schools and Movements
Thames & Hudson (2004)

De Noblet, J.
Industrial Design Reflection of a Century
Flammarion (1993)

Dixon, P.
Futurewise Six Faces of Global Change
Harper Collins (1998)

Fiell, C. and Fiell, P.
Design for the 21st Century
Taschen (2003)

Forty, A.
Objects of Desire
Thames & Hudson (1986)

Fuad-Luke, A.
The Eco-Design Handbook
Thames & Hudson (2002)

Fukasawa, N.
Naoto Fukasawa
Phaidon Press (2007)

Fulton Suri, J. and IDEO
Thoughtless Acts?
Chronicle Books (2005)

Gamper, M.
100 Chairs in 100 Days and its 100 Ways
Dent-De-Leone (2007)

Gershenfeld, N.
When Things Start to Think
Hodder & Stoughton (1999)

Hauffe, T.
Design A Concise History
Laurence King Publishing (1998)

Jensen, R.
The Dream Society
McGraw-Hill (1999)

Kaku, M.
Visions
Oxford University Press (1998)

Kelley, T.
The Ten Faces of Innovation
Doubleday (2005)

Lupton, E.
Skin
Laurence King Publishing (2002)

MacCarthy, F.
British Design Since 1880
Lund Humphries (1982)

Meneguzzo, M.
Philippe Starck Distordre
Electa/Alessi (1996)

Moors, A.
Simply Droog
Droog Design, revised edition (Jul 2006)

Papanek, V.
The Green Imperative
Thames & Hudson (1995)

Pink, D.
A Whole New Mind
Cyan (2005)

Smith, P.
You Can Find Inspiration in Everything
Violette Editions (2001)

Sozzani, F.
Kartell
Skira Editore Milan (2003)

Sweet, F.
Frog: Form Follows Emotion
Thames & Hudson Ltd (1999)

Thompson, D.
On Growth and Form
Cambridge University Press (1961)

Various
And Fork: 100 Designers, 10 Curators, 10 Good Designs
Phaidon Press Ltd (2007)

Walker, S.
Sustainable by Design – Explorations in Theory & Practice
Earthscan Ltd (2006)

Journals

Product Design WORLD
Abitare
Egg
MODO
ID
Metropolis magazine
Kult
FRUiTS
DEdiCate
frieze
dwell
icon
MONUMENT
!NNOVATION
vanidad
domus
wallpaper
TWILL
mix
newdesign
Design Week
AZURE
surface
FRAME
b0x
MARK
Design
intramuros
T3
Stuff
Blueprint
Artform
Lowdown
W magazine

Websites

www.core77.com
www.idsa.org
www.csd.org
www.designspotter.com
www.designmuseum.org
www.cooperhewitt.org
www.rsa.org.uk
www.newdesigners.com
www.cosmit.it
www.vam.ac.uk
www.TED.com
www.designboom.com

Contacts

www.animicausa.com
www.aqhayoncollection.com
www.bang-olufsen.com
www.barnabybarford.co.uk
www.braun.com
www.carlclerkin.co.uk
www.chihuly.com
www.colinbrownglass.co.uk
www.contact-design.com
www.droogdesign.nl
www.dyson.co.uk
www.ericmorel.com
www.frogdesign.com
www.gampermartino.com
www.geeksquad.com
www.gijsbakker.com
www.hayonstudio.com
www.hoshino-atr.com
www.ilviogallo.com
www.imagination.lancaster.ac.uk
www.industreal.it
www.kirkmikkelsen.com
www.kjamesphotography.com
www.ligne-roset.com
www.lincoln.ac.uk
www.lunar.com
www.makeupthe wall.com
www.marc-newson.com
www.merkok.com
www.metalarte.com
www.muji.com
www.nationalglasscentre.com
www.nikazupanc.com
www.nokia.com
www.norwaysays.com
www.oliver-schick.com
www.qed-design.de
www.qubus.cz
www.scienceandsons.com
www.smogmilano.com
www.stuarthaygarth.com
www.studiobramston.com
www.thorstenvanelten.com
www.tomvack.com
www.transalpin.net
www.verpan.dk
www.vliegervandam.com

Credits

Front Cover
Dave Bramston and Neil Housego

Pages 2–3
Stewart Bibby

Page 8
Tom Stott

Page 14
Dave Bramston

Page 15
Tim Harrison

Page 16
Dave Bramston and Neil Housego

Page 17
Clive McCarthy

Page 18 Panoramic montage
Tim Harrison

Page 18 Montage
Dave Overton

Page 19
Clive McCarthy

Page 20
Stewart Bibby

Page 21
Tim Harrison

Page 24
Clive McCarthy

Page 25
Philip Copland and Tim Harrison

Pages 26–27
Clive McCarthy

Pages 28–31
Dave Bramston

Pages 32–33
Clive McCarthy

Page 35 Margarine tub
Neil Housego

Page 35 Lorraine Lunch Bag
Angela Yoder

Page 36
Dyson

Page 37
Clive McCarthy

Pages 39–41
Clive McCarthy

Page 42
Tim Harrison

Page 43
Clive McCarthy

Page 44 When a ring is heard
Keith James

Page 44 Location at 2pm
Tim Harrison

Page 45
Clive McCarthy

Pages 46–47 Scrapbook
Dave Overton

Pages 48–49 Info dump
Tim Harrison and Stewart Bibby

Page 49 Journals
Dave Overton

Pages 50–51 Experiences
Peter Nunn

Page 51
Tim Harrison

Page 52
Michael Neubauer

Page 53
Shuya Sato

Page 55
Stewart Bibby

Pages 56–57
Tim Harrison

Page 58
Tim Harrison

Page 59
Clive McCarthy

Pages 60–62
Clive McCarthy

Page 64
Tim Harrison

Page 65
Clive McCarthy

Pages 66–67
Norway Says

Page 68 Themes
Michael Himpel

Page 69 Funghi
Mauricio Salinas

Page 69 The Pee Tree
Eric Morel

Contacts and credits

Page 70 Character
Justin Pipergen

Page 71 Character
Philip Sayer

Page 73
Neil Housego

Page 75
V Goico

Page 77
Stewart Bibby and Tim Harrison

Page 78
ArtQuitect

Page 81 Teapot
droog

Page 81 Guardian Angel
Vlieger & Vandam

Page 81 Foam Rose
Maria Kirk Mikkelsen

Page 82
Bjørn Blisse

Page 83
Stuart Haygarth

Pages 84–85
S.M.og Milano

Page 86
Clive McCarthy

Page 88
Dietmar Henneka

Page 89
Tim Harrison

Page 90
Ilvio Gallo

Page 91
Tristan Zimmermann

Pages 92–93
Terry Rishel

Pages 94–95
Russell Johnson

Page 97
Copyright Braun GmbH, Kronberg

Pages 99–103
Angus Mills and Åbäke

Page 104
Animi Causa

Page 107
Keith James

Page 108
Tom Vack

Pages 110 Beo Center 6
Søren Joneson/Bang & Olufsen
Mediacenter

Page 111 Serene Mobile
Jesper Jørgen/Bang & Olufsen
Mediacenter

Page 111 Beo Center 6
Søren Joneson/Bang & Olufsen
Mediacenter

Pages 112–113
Tim Harrison

Page 114
Vanessa Jesperson-Wheat

Page 115
Jim A Larsen

Pages 116–117
thorsten van elten

Page 118
Maria Kirk Mikkelsen

Page 119
Verner Panton

Page 121
Nokia

Page 122
Neil Housego

Page 125
Courtesy of Xavier Hufkens
Gallery

Pages 126–127
Mehmet Erkök

Pages 128–129
Nika Zupanc

Page 130
Stuart Walker

Pages 132–133
Tim Harrison

Page 134
Paul Loebach

Page 135
Thomas Dobbie

Page 136
Clive McCarthy

Page 138
Julia Kopelson

Page 139
Wouter Geense Design Studio

Pages 140–142
Clive McCarthy

Page 143
Stewart Bibby

Page 145
Tom Stott

Page 147
Geek Squad

Page 149
Tim Harrison

Pages 150–151
Stuart Walker

Page 153
Alessi S.p.a.

Page 166
Tim Harrison

Definitions taken from the
*Concise Oxford English
Dictionary.*

Acknowledgements

Thank you to all the designers, artists, photographers and researchers who have supported this project and provided exciting images and statements. The information has been sourced from all over the world and has involved young designers along with influential leaders within their respective disciplines. The involvement of all of these individuals is really appreciated.

Many thanks to the Product Design staff and students at the University of Lincoln (UK) who have helped tremendously with the project. The understanding and willingness to get involved is also very much appreciated and respected.

Thank you to Sarah Jameson for the continued efforts in ensuring that requested images were located and included and also thank you to Malcolm Southward for the book design.

Finally it is important to recognise and thank the staff at AVA publishing and in particular Caroline Walmsley, Lucy Tipton and Brian Morris who identified the project and provided the opportunity, the necessary support and drive for the book.